Understanding Halakhic Man

A Commentary and Companion Guide to the Essay

By Rabbi Richard Borah

In memory of my parents Harry & Judith Borah, zt'l

Thanks and appreciation:

To my wife Andrea for her patience and support and to my Rebbeim who have given me the Torah, life's most precious gift.

To Caryn Liebman for her important assistance.

Better is one hour of Torah and mitzvot in this world than the whole life of the world to come (Avot: 4:17)

Copyright © 2018 Richard Borah
Published by Observant Artist Community Circle
All rights reserved
ISBN-10: 0692188401
ISBN-13-978-0692188408

Table of Contents*

Understanding Halakhic Man
A Commentary and Companion Guide to the Essay

By Rabbi Richard Borah

*Chapter Numbers are from the original Essay
 Sub-Heading Titles are from the Author

Introduction 6

Part One: Halakhic Man: His World View and His Life 10

Chapter One 11
Rabbi Soloveitchik's Use of the Pure Ideal Type 12
The Role of Conflict in the Halakhic Man 13

Chapter Two 19
Introduction to Cognitive Man 19
Introduction to *Homo Religiosus* 22

Chapter Three 25
The Knowable Nature of Reality 30
Homo Religiosus Senses What Cannot be Cognized 32

Chapter Four 37
The Homo Religiosus in Science and Philosophy 40
Varieties of *Homo Religiosus* and Their Practices 41

Chapter Five 43
Cognitive Man's Dual Relationship with Reality 44

Chapter Six 52
The Breadth of Halakhic Application 55

Chapter Seven 61
Halakhic Man's Perspective on Death 63
Torah is For Man, Not Angels 66
The Paramount Value of Life in Halakhah 67
Halakhic Man's Fear of Death 69
The Transformation of the Mind and Personality by the Halakhah 70
The Higher Longs for the Lower 71

Chapter Eight 73
The Courage and Fortitude of Halakhic Man 74
Is Homo Religiosus Making A Mistake in His Method of Serving God? 76
The Exoteric Nature of Halakhic Man 77
Halakhic Man and the Concept of Holiness 80

Chapter Nine 83
The Mystic's Perspective of Tzimtzum 84
The "Tragic Trade-off" Necessary to Allow the Existence of the World 86
The Mystic's Longing for the End of the Existence 87
The Ultimate Antinomy of God and Creation 88
Halakhic Man's Unambivalent Embrace of God's Creation 88
The Creation of the World as God's Will 90
Halakhah and the Concretizing of Infinity 93
Halakhic Quantification of Reality and *Tzimtzum* 92
The Two Dimension of Creation That are Subject to Quantification 94
Rabbi Soloveitchik's Criticism of Maimonides View of *Piyyutim* 95
The Halakhah and the Structuring of the Human Inner Experience 96

Chapter Ten 100

Chapter Eleven 104
The Tragic Aspect of the *Homo Religiosus* 105

Chapter Twelve 110
Rav Hayyim and Rabbi Salanter – A Meeting of Halakhic Man and *Homo Religiosus* 112
Halakhic Man's State of Equilibrium 113

Chapter Thirteen 114
The "Self" of Halakhic Man and *Homo Religiosus* 116
The Intellect of Halakhic Man and *Homo Religiosus* 116
The Humility of *Homo Religiosus* and Halakhic Man 116
The Creative Role of Halakhic Man 118

Chapter Fourteen 121
The Religious Ecstasy of Halakhic Man 121
The "Sin" of Overlooking the Particulars 123
How Halakhah Deepens the Religious Experience for Halakhic Man 124
Halakhic Man – A Man of Few Words 125
Halakhic Man's Learning Torah *Lishmah* 126

Chapter Fifteen 128
Halakhic Man – Consistent, Courageous and Just 128
Halakhic Man Places No Objective Above Halakhah 129
The Profound Courage of Halakhic Man 129
The Moral Consistency of Halakhic Man 130

Part II Halakhic Man: His Creative Capacity 133

Halakhic Man Part Two-Introduction 134

Chapter One 136
Obedient Creativity 136
The Halakhic Nature of the Entire Torah 137
God's "Creation of Chaos" in the World 140

Chapter Two 144
Creativity, Holiness and the Blessing on the New Moon 144
How Man "Atones" for God 146
Creativity and the Realization of Holiness 147
Halakhah = Contraction=Holiness=Creation 148

Man as the Source of Holiness and Chaos and the Creator of Himself 149

Chapter Three 151
Creativity and Repentance 151
The Creative Gesture of Repentance 155
Repentance of Halakhic Man Differs from that of *Homo Religiosus* 156
Repentance and the Halakhic Man's View of Time 157
Creativity and Causality 159

Chapter Four 161
Time and the Experiencing of the *Masorah* 163
Fleeting Time vs. Eternal Time 163

Chapter Five 166
The Obligation to be Under God's Providence 171

Chapter Six 172
Maimonides Depiction of Man's Creativity as a Departure from Aristotle 174
The Halakhah's Valuing & Validation of the Individual 175
Self-Creation & Liberation from the Universal 176
Free Will, Halakhah and the Creative Process 178

Introduction

The essay "Halakhic Man" was written in 1944 by Rabbi Joseph B. Soloveitchik, one of the leading orthodox rabbinic authorities of the twentieth century. Rabbi Soloveitchik (often referred to as simply "the Rav"- a term we will use extensively in referring to him) received his Doctorate from the Friedrich Wilheim University in Berlin Germany in December of 1932, writing his Ph.D thesis on the epistemology and metaphysics of the philosophy of Herman Cohen. By 1941 Rabbi Soloveitchik succeeded his father at the RIETS rabbinical school of Yeshiva University where he taught until 1986. During his tenure he ordained over 2,000 rabbis and was universally acknowledged as the definitive scholar of American modern orthodoxy. The text of "Halakhic Man" was translated from its original Hebrew language version (*Ish Halakhahh*) into an English text by Lawrence Kaplan. This translation was carried out under the guidance of Rabbi Soloveitchik himself. The English version was completed and published in 1983, with the Rav's approval. In the current book we will be utilizing this English version of "Halakhic Man" for our analysis and cited quotes.

In the 35 years since the publication of its English version, "Halakhic Man" has continued to grow in stature and impact and currently stands as one of the few contemporary philosophically-oriented texts by an orthodox Jewish rabbi that has achieved such an enduring level of distinction and focus for scholars, rabbis and the general public. The essay has helped to shape and articulate a contemporary understanding of the underlying nature of the Halakhah (Jewish law) and of those unique individuals who have dedicated themselves wholly to its study and realization.

The current work will attempt provide a chapter by chapter guide to the English language "Halakhic Man" text. Although the Rav is a truly magnificent writer who achieves an almost poetic level of expression at times, he is also difficult to comprehend due to the depth of his ideas and the varied Jewish and general references he utilizes in the essay and its extensive footnotes. I hope to be of particular assistance to those struggling with more cryptic portions of the essay, while also providing some background and insight on each of the issues the Rav raises. I have proceeded with the assumption that the reader has a limited level of understanding of traditional Jewish learning methodologies and Jewish law and is not fully versed in the philosophical and scientific ideas and concepts which Rabbi Soloveitchik incorporates into his explanations.

My hope in writing this guide is to increase the number of people who will be able to appreciate the important ideas expressed in *Halackhic Man* and obtain a deeper insight and appreciation of the Halakhic system of laws and learning. Another central objective of "Halakhic Man" is to clarify how the halakhah can have a potentially transformative impact on one who places it at the center of his or her thoughts and actions. The current guide will focus on helping to elucidate the Rav's depiction of this unique path of human metamorphosis.

The Text Format

The Essay "Halakhic Man" is divided into two parts by Rabbi Soloveitchik:

Part One: "Halakhic Man: His World View and His Life"- Part One is divided into 15 chapters.
Part Two: "Halakhic Man: His Creative Capacity"- Part Two is divided into 6 chapters.

Following the text of the essay are 147 footnotes, many of which are brief explanatory essays in their own right. We will follow the parts and chapters of *Halakhic Man's* format in our own present guide with Part 1 presented in 15 chapters and Part 2 divided into 6 chapters. Some, but not all of the footnotes will be explained along with the texts which they are clarifying.

I should add that, unfortunately, I did not have the benefit of learning with Rabbi Soloveitchik or of sharing my reflections about "Halakhic Man" with him. My thoughts and explanations are my own and, of course, will be flawed to the extent that I am unable to truly understand the ideas put forth by one of the Jewish people's greatest minds. Even those ideas that I may understand to some degree, I may be unsuccessful in communicating accurately or lucidly. In spite of these limitations, I still have decided to do my best to try and help others understand an essay that has become so central to my own appreciation of the exalted nature of the halakhah, and of the personality and motivation of the Torah scholar. By gaining a clear understanding of these specifically Jewish areas of knowledge, I believe one also obtains more general insights regarding the nature of knowledge and of human thought in a more general manner.

Many of the insight utilized in this book were developed during years of teaching classes in "Halakhic Man" at the Masoret Institute for Higher Jewish Learning in Inwood, New York. This school provided classes in a variety of Jewish areas for adult women interested in an intensive level of study. I would like to thank the Director of the Masoret Institute, Rabbi Reuven Mann, for the opportunity to teach the Rav's work to these students.

Rabbi Richard Borah, October, 2018

Understanding Halakhic Man

Part I

His World View and His Life

Part One: Halakhic Man: His World View and His Life

Chapter One

In the first chapter of Part One the author starts to bring into the focus the term "halakhic man" and the personality of this unique individual. He is certainly much more than a person who follows Jewish Law, which is also known as "the Halakhah". The term "*halakhah*" in Hebrew is rooted in the Hebrew verb *halach* (*hay, lamid, chet,*) which is translated as "to go" or "to walk". The "*halakhah*" is the "operating system" of the observant Jew-the way an observant Jew "goes or does" in a myriad of legislated Torah and rabbinic rulings that cover every aspect of life from the most mundane to the most exalted. When an observant Jews want to know whether something is permissible or prohibited, or whether it is recommended or discouraged by the body of Jewish legal decision, he or she will inquire of a Rav or a text, "What is the halakhah regarding this issue?" However, as we stated earlier, "halakhic man" means something much more than simply a person who follows the *halakhah* as the guiding system for his day to day and life decisions.

The Rav does not attempt to directly define the halakhic man in this first chapter. Instead he begins by clarifying what he is not. He is not what the Rav terms "homo religious". He is not what the Rav terms "cognitive man". However, halakhic man does contain certain elements of both these types within his unique amalgam. He will describe both cognitive man and *homo religiosus* in some detail. The Rav uses the term "anti-nomic" to describe halakhic man. Anti-nomic is the adjective form of the term "antinomy" which is defined as follows: "a fundamental and apparently unresolvable conflict or contradiction". An anti-nomic persona would then be one in which there are at least two parts which, though co-existing, do not result in a single, unified whole. This quality, the Rav attributes, to halakhic man. Rabbi Soloveitchik states:

> Halakhic man is an anti-nomic type for a dual reason: (1) he bears within the deep recesses of his personality the soul of *homo religious*, that soul which, as was stated above, suffers from the pangs of self-contradiction and self-negation; (2) at the same time halakhic man's personality also embraces the soul of cognitive man, and this soul contradicts all of these desires and strivings of the religious consciousness. (HM, p. 3-4)

Rabbi Soloveitchik's Use of the Pure Ideal Type

In the first note at the end of "Halakhic Man" the Rav explains that when he employs the terms halakhic man, cognitive man or *homo religious* he is describing a pure ideal type. In order to make clear the qualities and distinct features of each of these personas he presents them as if there are people who are 100% halakhic man and nothing else or 100% *homo religious* and nothing else. The same technique is used for describing cognitive man. In reality though, the Rav explains that people are hybrids of these pure types. I suppose if a particular individual needed to be categorized as to which of these three types he belonged, one would do so by the one that is most dominant and definitive in his view of the world and his objectives. But no one is absolutely 100% of one type to the exclusion of all characteristics of the others. The Rav writes:

> Obviously the description of halakhic man given here refers to a pure ideal type, as is the case with the other types with which the human sciences (*geisteswissenschaften*) are concerned. Real halakhic men, who are not simple but rather hybrid types, approximate, to a lesser or greater degree, the ideal halakhic man, each in accordance with his spiritual image and stature. (H.M. Notes Part One, Note #1, p. 139)

The Role of Conflict in the Halakhic Man

The Rav will provide clarifications of each of the two personae, *homo religious* and cognitive man as we proceed. But a point that Rabbi Soloveitchik wants to make strongly at the outset is that the seemingly contradictory elements that reside within the personality of the halakhic man are not a disability or a situation which diminishes his capacity to achieve clarity, insight and closeness to God. He states:

> However, these opposing forces which struggle together in the religious consciousness of halakhic man are not of a destructive or disjunctive nature. Halakhic man is not some illegitimate, unstable hybrid. On the contrary, out of the contradictions and antinomies there emerges a radiant, holy personality whose soul has been purified in the furnace of struggle and opposition and redeemed in the fires of the torments of spiritual disharmony to a degree unmatched by the universal homo religious. The deep split of the soul prior to its being united may, at times, raise a man to a rank of perfection, which for sheer brilliance and beauty is unequaled by any level attained by a simple, whole personality who has never been tried by the pangs of spiritual discord. (HM, p. 4)

The Rav has not yet delved into the nature of this internal conflict that rages within the soul of halakhic man. As it is due to his having dimensions of both the homo religious and the cognitive man, the Rav must first describe these two pure types in some detail. This he does in Chapters 2 through 5. But at this early point in the essay is it important to point out the central role of conflict in the Rav's conception of the human soul's development.

The Rav is passionate about shattering the popular view of religion as a peaceful path through which one escapes the harshness and cruelty of the world and retreats into a personal paradise where one can feel safe, content and complete. Rabbi Soloveitchik virtually rages against this perspective, which is widely held by both the religionists themselves and by those who see religious people as indulging in an attempt to escape the stark realities and difficulties of life. The Rav, on the other hand, exalts in conflict! He views the embrace of conflict as the only path to spiritual growth and a meaningful religious life. The Rav writes:

> ...there is a creative power embedded in antithesis; conflict enriches existence, the negation constructive, and contradiction deepens and expands the ultimate destiny of both man and the world. (HM, p. 4)

The Rav expounds on this utter rejection of the gentle, peaceful religious path to enlightenment in Note 4 following the essay. In this expansive and intense explanation, Rabbi Soloveitchik makes clear the folly and destructiveness of viewing the religious life "as a poetic Arcadia, a realm of simplicity, wholeness and tranquility". He writes:

> ...This popular ideology contends that the religious experience is tranquil and neatly ordered, tender and delicate; it is an enchanted stream for embittered souls and still waters for troubled spirits. The person "who comes in

> from the field, weary" (Gen. 25:29 (which is filled with doubts and fears, contradictions and refutations, clings to religion as does a baby to its mother and finds in her lap "a shelter for his head, the nest of his forsaken prayers" –H.N. Bialik "Hakhnisini tahat kenafekh" - and there is comforted for his disappointments and tribulations…(HM, Note #4, p. 140)

The Rav continues in a derisive fashion, disdainful of those who would embrace such a false approach to spiritual developments. He writes:

> If you wish to achieve a fine psychic equilibrium without have to first undergo a slow, gradual personal development, turn unto religion. And if you wish to achieve an instant spiritual wholeness and simplicity that need not be forged out of the struggles and torments of consciousness, turn unto religion!...There is no need for a process of transition with all its torments and upheavals. A person can acquire spiritual tranquility in a single moment. (Ibid)

Rabbi Soloveitchik continues to explain in this note that not only is this approach to religious life empty and without true development, it is also a highly destructive path for the individual and the society. He sees this retreat to a quiet, tranquil religious plane as a retreat from inquiry, introspection and knowledge itself. It leads to what the Rav sees as an almost diabolical Romanticism in which people believe what they want to believe because it is emotionally appealing. For the Rav, conflict is the necessary result of one who truly explores and reflects upon the world and oneself. To avoid conflict one must avoid honesty and flee from a dedication to truthfulness and accuracy. He explains:

> The individual who frees himself from the rational principle and who casts off the yoke of objective thought will in the end turn destructive and lay waste the entire created order. Therefore it is preferable that religion should ally itself for the forces of clear, logical cognition, as uniquely exemplified in the scientific method, even though at time the two might clash with one another, rather than pledge its troth to beclouded, mysterious ideologies that grope in dark corners of existence, unaided by the shining light of objective knowledge, and believe that they have penetrated to the secret core of the world. (HM, p. 141)

It is not clear to me who exactly is the focus of the Rav's ridicule in this note. It is not the *homo religious* who, as the Rav describes later in the same note, embraces conflict in his process of growth. It is certainly not the cognitive man, whose rationality is praised by Rabbi Soloveitchik here as a better model for the religious person's approach than what the Rav sees as a highly emotional, self-indulgent approach of the escapist religionist. He is equally scornful of any person (he lists a number of renowned philosophers including Bergson, Nietzsche, Spengler, Klages, and Heidegger) who indulges in viewing reality through an irrational lens of their own intuitive preference. The Rav sees these thinkers along with the simple soul who seek to retreat into a religious paradise, as sharing a common flaw of emotional and intellectual self-indulgence. Both types, in their own way, indulge a desire to achieve spiritual bliss without going through the torturous gauntlet of self-creation and development. He explains:

> And, second, this ideology is intrinsically false and deceptive. That religious consciousness in man's experience which is

most profound and most elevated, which penetrates to the very depths and ascends to the very heights, is not that simple and comfortable. On the contrary, it is exceptionally complex, rigorous, and tortuous. Where you find its complexity, there you find its greatness. (HM, p. 141)

In concluding this powerful exposition, the Rav does accept the idea that a tranquility and wholeness can eventually be achieved by the religious person. But this is only after he has gone through the redeeming process of embracing and wrestling with conflicts. He concludes:

> The pangs of searching and groping, the tortures of spiritual crises and exhausting treks of the soul purify and sanctify man, cleanse his thoughts, and purge them of the husks of superficiality and the dross of vulgarity. Out of these torments there emerges a new understanding of the world, a powerful spiritual enthusiasm that shakes the very foundations of man's existence. He arises from the agonies purged and refined, possessed of a pure heart and a new spirit...The spiritual stature and countenance of the man of God are chiseled and formed by the pangs of redemption themselves. (HM, p. 143)

The first chapter of "Halakhic Man" concludes with a brief description of halakhic man as:

> this "strange singular" being who reveals himself to the world from within his narrow, constricted "four cubits" (Berakhot 8a) his hands soiled by the gritty realia of practical Halakhah (See Barekhot 4a).

This initial thumbnail sketch of halakhic man may seem to portray him as somewhat small and insignificant ("narrow, constricted") . We will see how the Rav develops this sketch into a detailed and subtle portrait of a heroic individual who is noble, wise and courageous. I believe that a major objective of the essay is to dispel the common misunderstanding of the casual observer who assesses the halakhic scholar to be a pedantic, person who sees nothing in life beyond the decision of what is permitted and what is prohibited by the law. Many may mistakenly conclude that the Talmudic sage lacks any true depth or a sense of the "bigger picture". The essay continues in the next chapter with a description of the two alter-egos of the halakhic man: cognitive man and *homo religious*.

Chapter Two

In the second chapter of "Halakhic Man", Part One the essay delves into the underlying natures of *homo religious* and cognitive man. The Rav's approach is to define each of these pure types by contrasting one to the other. His analysis does not concentrate on the external differences of the two types, such as lifestyle or religious affiliation. Instead, he focuses on the contrasting internal states of the *homo religious* and cognitive man and the different dimensions of reality which interests and motivates their thoughts and actions.

Introduction to Cognitive Man

Cognitive man's nature is easier to understand than that of *homo religiosus*. This is because cognitive man has a clearly defined objective and precise methodology of achieving it. The cognitive man is interested in understanding the physical world in order to master those aspects of the environment that can be understood, controlled and utilized to improve the quality of human life. The Rav states:

> When cognitive man observes and scrutinizes the great and exalted cosmos, it is with the intent of understanding and comprehending its features; cognitive man's desire is to uncover the secret of the world and to unravel the problems of existence. When theoretical and scientific man peers into the cosmos, he is filled with one exceedingly powerful yearning, which is to search for clarity and understanding, for solutions and resolutions. (HM, p. 5)

The Rav identifies cognitive man with the intellectual quest to understand the structure and laws that underlie the physical world. Cognitive man has no interest in reflecting on the particular, individual phenomena he encounters. His sole focus is on the general laws and objective aspects of the world around him. This type of intellectual focus follows from the legacy of Plato and Aristotle, as Rabbi Soloveitchik writes:

> Any phenomenon which cannot be subjected to the rule of law and principle is relegated to the realm of the nonbeing and nothingness of the Platonists or, at best, to the hylic matter posited by Aristotle. The common denominator of both the Platonic and Aristotelian views is that the random and the particular are not deemed worthy of being granted the status of the real and the existent and remain in the realm of chaos and the void. Only that which is engraved with the imprint of lawful reality merits the appellation and title of true and effective being in which the idea participates. (HM, p. 5-6)

Which individuals would be found under the rubric of cognitive man? Certainly the scientist and the engineer are of this type. But more generally it applies to any person who is attempting to find the general principle behind a number of individual phenomena. How does something work? Why do people react in a certain way to certain situations? A physicist studying the movements of the stars, a physician studying how the human body operates or the psychologist studying the different types of mental states of adolescents all are examples of cognitive man. The interest is not in the individual case, but how the individual case is representative of a general category. Every "*ologist*" from anthropologist to zoologist would be full-fledged examples of cognitive man.

All of us, regardless of what we do for a living, look at the world through the eyes of cognitive man when we are engaged in the process of understanding or discovering a general principle beyond a number of individual events. As a child we begin to form working principles and rules that can be applied in a general way. If a throw something up it will come back down. I take individual cases of throwing things up and see that each of them comes down. I create a generalized principle. This is cognitive man (or cognitive child) in action. I may delve deeper into this phenomenon to try to understand it more precisely and observe that things fall more quickly the longer they fall. I might take it to the next level and measure the falling object as descending at 32 feet per second by end of the first second, 64 feet per second at the end of the next second and continuing to accelerate at this rate as the object falls. I may study mathematics and physics and learn the equation for the acceleration of a falling object is

Acceleration falling object = $\frac{2 \times \text{distance the object falls}}{\text{the time the object falls}}$
   ($a=2d/t$)

These are stages of cognitive man's inquiry, beginning with the child's simple conclusion and developing towards the precise, mathematical formulation of the natural law. The human mind has this exalted ability to discovery and understand general principles about the world in which it lives. The Rav concludes here:

> No matter how diverse these various concepts of causality are, they all reveal the basic tendency of cognitive man: the search for the ordered and fixed in existence….Cognition for him, consists in discovering the secret, solving the riddle, hidden buried deep in reality, precisely through the cognition of the scientific order and pattern of the world. (HM, p.6)

Introduction to *Homo Religiosus*

The essay continues with a description of *homo religiosus* (religious man). Here the analysis focuses as much on what *homo religiosus* is not, as much as on what he is. The Rav begins:

> The homo religiosus acts differently. When he confronts God's world, when he gazes at the myriads of events and phenomena occurring in the cosmos, he does not desire to transform the secrets embedded in creation into simple equations that a mere tyro (novice-RB) is capable of grasping. On the contrary, *homo religiosus* is intrigued by the mystery of existence-the *mysterium tremendum*-and wants to emphasize that mystery. He gazes at that which is obscure without the intent of explaining it and inquires into that which is concealed without the intent of receiving the reward of a clear understanding. (HM, 6-7)

So the first thing we can say about *homo religiosus* is that he does not view the hidden, unknown aspects of the world around him as a problem to be solved. For cognitive man the unknown is the opponent, so to speak, that has to be subdued through study, observation and reflection, to yield its secrets. The *homo religiosus* experiences the unknown, mysterious elements of the world as exhilarating and one which focuses his attention on this unknowable dimension which he finds meaningful. The Rav states:

> He gazes at that which is obscure without the intent of explaining it and inquires into that which is concealed without the intent of receiving the reward of a clear understanding. (HM, p. 7)

The Rav clarifies that cognitive man does not reject the study and discerning of the orderly and lawful in the world.

However, while discovering the underlying generalizable nature of phenomena is the end point for cognitive, for *homo religiosus*, these discoveries only deepen and intensify the mysterious dimension of things that remains sealed, through hinted at by that which is knowable.

> *Homo religiosus*, like cognitive man seeks the lawful and the ordered, the fixed and the necessary. But for the former, unlike the latter, the revelation of the law and the comprehension of the order and interconnectedness of existence only intensifies and deepens the question and the problem...For to him the concept of lawfulness is in itself the deepest of mysteries. (HM, p. 7)

The Rav does not explain precisely what is the mystery or mysteries that so enthralls *homo religiosus*. We can speculate at this point. Rabbi Soloveitchik does clarify that it is the study and discerning of the knowable aspects of the world that stimulate the *homo religiosus's* sense of the unknowable. We will delve more deeply into this experience in the next chapter. Let's conclude here with the point that cognitive man and *homo religiosus* view the unlocking of the knowable secrets of the world that reveal themselves through cognition (reason, analysis, induction, deduction) as different acts. For cognitive man this unlocking is the be all and end all of his quest. He has dug and found the treasure. For *homo religiosus,* every discovery of the knowable intensifies the sense and awareness of the inherently unknowable dimension of the world.

I will attempt a *mushal* (analogous story) and an example from the development of physics to clarify how discovery can deepen the mystery of a phenomenon instead of reducing the mystery First the *mushal*. I land on the planet Mars and I find a clay pot under five inches of Martian dust. The pot looks similar to the pots that house plants are placed in on Earth. It has a blue glaze on it. This is a mystery. Upon closer examination I read an inscription on the bottom of the pot. It says, "made in New Jersey". This additional information only increases the level of the mystery. Now will we illustrate the concept using an example from the development of physics.

In the history of physics there have been a number of pivotal discoveries that have increased our understanding of certain phenomena, but which in turn created a greater level of mystery about the overall structure of the physical world. Perhaps the most dramatic of these discoveries was the development of quantum mechanics which, though providing a much greater understanding of the pattern of subatomic particle movement, simultaneously undermined the principles of causation and the movement of objects through space which were previously among the most fundamental assumptions about the nature of the physical world. It introduced probability and randomness as fundamental characteristics of nature, creating a profound mystery regarding an imaginable mechanism for the movement of atomic and subatomic particles. Knowledge which intensifies mystery is how *homo religiosus* views the progress made in the discovery of the world's knowable dimension. In the next chapter Rabbi Soloveitchik will explain, in greater depth, how the world's dual aspect– being both discoverable and eternally hidden, reflects the dual perspectives of cognitive man and *homo religiosus*.

Chapter Three

Rabbi Soloveitchik explains what he calls the two-fold nature of existence. The study of the nature of existence (ontology/ontological) has two distinct and disparate approaches as we've described: 1) the discovery of the knowable, understandable dimension of existence by cognitive man and 2) the exalting in the unknowable by *homo religiosus*. This, the Rav explains, reflects the two-fold nature of reality itself, which he terms "ontic dualism". "Ontic" is defined by Webster's as "relating to or having real being". The Rav writes, quite poetically:

> Reality possesses two faces. On the one hand, she presents us with a bright, happy, smiling face; she greets us with a cheerful countenance and reveals to us something of her essence. She shows us a bit of her lawful structure and the order of her actions. In such moments of grace and compassion the object submits itself to the subject, the thing to the person, reality-to man who forms an inextricable part of it, existence-to intellect and knowledge. Here there blossoms forth the wondrous relationship between subject and object, cognizer and cognized. The process of cognition, the problems and enigma of enigmas of man, reveals itself in all its splendor and majesty. And it is this act of grace, this act of disclosure, which nature, at times, performs for our benefit, that is at the root of all human culture.

Here Rabbi Soloveitchik conveys the world of cognitive man. He describes that aspect of the world which is understandable through observation and rational, intellectual analysis. This includes all aspects of man's understanding and mastery of his environment. How to utilize materials to build and construct things. How to manipulate matter and energy to produce things. How to discern to characteristics of things and, in many cases, apply these characteristics to address human need and desire. This is what the Rav explains as "this act of grace, this act of disclosure, which nature, at times, performs for our benefit, that is at the root of all human culture". All those things in the world which we can clear understanding of things through observation and analysis fall under this category of the "revealed"

The revealed dimension of the world is paralleled by the concealed one. That human beings are capable of understanding the world and make progress in mastering certain areas of knowledge for their benefit and clarification is not difficult to grasp. Especially in contemporary times where the impact of technology on our daily lives seems to grow daily, this aspect of the world is abundantly apparent. It is the "concealed face" of the world which is much more difficult to grasp and to give its due as a source of man's knowledge of the world and his perspective. It is this equally important dimension of existence, which is, by its nature, much less describable or able to be concretely clarified. It is more expressed in the psalm that the essay, in silence more than speech, in the private internal experience than in the shared generalizable qualities of a phenomenon. The Rav begins his description of the concealed dimension of reality using anthropomorphic language with reality depicted as a modest woman:

> On the other hand, however, reality is possessed on an extreme modesty; at times she conceals herself in her innermost chamber and disappears from the view of the

scholar and investigator. Everything bespeaks secrets and enigmas, everything-wonders and miracles. (HM, p. 8)

The Rav continues with the idea that as the human investigator discovers more of the revealed reality of the world, he is faced with a deeper, clearer sense of the concealed and that one's sense of the vastness and depth of the concealed dimension of reality increased exponentially. He writes:

> And reality is characterized by a strange feature. For, at the very moment when she treats us generously and reveals to us a bit of her form, she covers much more. The problem increases as the cognition progresses. (HM, p. 8)

Here we should pause and dig in a bit into the nature of this expanding mystery. As I see it there are two distinct types of mystery. The solvable mystery and the unsolvable one. Certain areas of the concealed dimension of existence are inherently so and others are potentially revealable with cognitive creativity, time and effort. Which of these is the Rav referring to here? Or perhaps he is referring to both types? An expanding mystery which is still of the potentially revealable type would be those scientific discoveries which when explaining the underlying pattern of a particular phenomenon, reveal the existence of another phenomenon or group of phenomena which are not understood and are even more fundamental to the system than the original phenomenon that was explained. This has occurred often in the history of the sciences.

In the 1600's, the compound microscope was developed and people discovered that living tissue was composed of small distinct components we call "cells". This revelation opened up a vast area of mystery as there was a whole new area of knowledge that was wholly unexplored and yet was the underlying structure of all living things. Here a bit was revealed which also revealed a greater mystery. When improvements in the telescope revealed the presence of billions of galaxies and a much larger observable universe than was previously known, we have another example where a discovery reveals a much greater mystery. But in these cases and cases like them, the vast mystery revealed is still able to be revealed by continued study.

In the type of discoveries and new mysteries described above, cognitive man is still in control and on the path of further discovery. In current times, many of the mysteries of the original viewers of cells have been discerned. Scientists continue to study the nature of the expanded universe that improved telescopes have revealed. It may be true that as cognitive explorers solve one problem multiple cognizable problems emerge and that this is fundamental to the nature of the world. The Rav seems to imply that this was the position of Neo-Kantian philosopher Herman Cohen (the focus of the Rav's philosophy PhD thesis). The Rav states in the tenth note following the text:

> ...For the neo-Kantians, the problem does not express itself in concealing and hiding but rather in creating and revealing. The process of cognition does not conceal, but creates and discloses. Both the problem itself and the unending task constitute an essential part of the process of the unfolding and "creation" of the logos, for is it not the case that there is no existence without cognition? Even in Hermann Cohen's first period when the absolute still appeared-to be sure only qua task and not qua given-the riddle which surpasses cognition did not enter his rationalist outlook....*Homo religiosus*

"senses" a problem that was not created by the logos but that exists eternally without any relationship to cognition. The religious riddle is transcendent, sealed and opaque. (HM, Note #10, p. 144)

The rationalist who sees cognition as the sole method of acquiring knowledge, it seems, may propound the idea that the nature of the world is such that the field of cognitive inquiry continues to grow with each discovery. However, the rationalist approach, of which cognitive man is a proponent, still limits all knowledge to that which is revealable. He does not accept or, at least, does not concern himself with the world of the inherently concealed- that aspect of reality which can be sensed but not known- which reveals a profound, essential dimension of existence but which is not subject to cognition. Let's now try to make some progress describing this inherent mystery and the one that truly to interest of *homo religiosus* As the Rav describes it:

> He (*homo religiosus*) clings to a reality which, as it were, has removed itself from the cognizing subject and has barred the intellect from all access to it. He is totally devoted and given over to a cosmos that is filled with divine secrets and eternal mysteries. The very nature of the law itself, the very phenomenon of cognition is an open book for cognitive man and a closed one for homo religiosus. (HM, p.9)

Here we are not describing concealed phenomena that are potentially revealable through the efforts of continued cognitive efforts. The concealment here is inherent to the nature of the phenomenon itself and is "not subject to cognition". It is the difference between the unknowable and the unknown. But, we can ask, are we limited to the a negative knowledge of this area of reality – simply describing what it is not? Are words completely useless in the description of this dimension of existence? What is the nature of the "eternally concealed" nature of existence which enthralls and beckons *homo religiosus*. Rabbi Soloveitchik states:

> The very nature of the law itself, the very phenomenon of cognition is an open book for cognitive man and a closed one for *homo religiosus*. (HM, p.9)

The Knowable Nature of Reality

The human mind has a profound ability to understand the underlying mechanisms that organize matter, energy and time. This knowledge is not limited to functional knowledge which improves our survivability as a species. Though it is certainly true that our intellectual ability to fashion tools, plant crops, and create shelter against the elements, provide significant practical benefits, the human mind's ability to understand the patterns of nature far exceeds this limited scope. The almost boundless nature of human cognition has become more and more apparent as scientific and technical progress has continued at an accelerating pace. Recent discoveries in astronomy and physics have revealed the fundamental nature of space, time and matter. Human cognition has revealed itself as capable of discovering the deepest secrets of the physical universe.

Albert Einstein, whose theories of special and general relativity are among mankind's most profound cognitive feats, famously noted the mysterious and wondrous nature of human cognition. He stated:

> The most incomprehensible thing about the world is that it is comprehensible. "Physics and Reality"(1936), in *Ideas and Opinions*, trans. Sonja Bargmann (New York: Bonanza, 1954), p292.

Einstein expounded on this idea in a letter to a philosophy student, Maurice Solovine:

> You find it strange that I consider the comprehensibility of the world (to the extent that we are authorized to speak of such a comprehensibility) as a miracle or as an eternal mystery. Well, *a priori*, one should expect a chaotic world, which cannot be grasped by the mind in any way... the kind of order created by Newton's theory of gravitation, for example, is wholly different. Even if a man proposes the axioms of the theory, the success of such a project presupposes a high degree of ordering of the objective world, and this could not be expected *a priori*. That is the 'miracle' which is constantly reinforced as our knowledge expands.

Ironically, perhaps history's greatest "cognitive man" is expressing here a perspective that closely parallels that of the Rav's *homo religiosus*. But as we stated earlier, the Rav understands that people are hybrids of these pure types and Einstein was obviously deeply rooted as both a cognitive man and a *homo religiosus*, at least with regard to his great wonder at the human ability to understand the world. As Einstein writes "*apriori* one should expect a chaotic world, which cannot be grasped by the mind in any way". The term "*apriori*" is usually defined as "prior to experience" or "what I would have concluded without any external information".

The *Homo Religiosus* Senses What Cannot be Cognized

We have to ask what is the objective of the *homo religiosus* when he cognizes and experiences the world? It is to understand clearly how he does not understand the underlying essence and foundation of the existence that he observes and studies. No matter how much he discerns about the cognizable dimension of the world, it will only come to strengthen his conviction that the underlying foundations of existence upon which the cognizable emanate from are absolutely unknowable. As cognitive man reveals the amazing scope and perfect order of the cognizable world he will long more and more to understand how such a thing could come to be and that there is a deeper more fundamental and true reality upon which it depends. His awe and mystery of this unknowable realm will grow with his knowledge of the knowable. So while the cognitive man cognizes to deepen and broaden his understanding of the knowable dimension of existence, *homo religiosus* cognizes with the objective of intensifying his sense of that which cannot be cognized.

Surprisingly, Rabbi Soloveitchik brings Maimonides and his methodology of understanding God through negative theology as an example of *homo religiosus*'s process of utilizing cognition to clarify that more fundamental and true knowledge that is not subject to cognition. Negative theology, according to Maimonides is an orderly, logical process by which one removes from one's concept of God those characteristics which exist in created being but not the Creator. For example, God lacks, one body and all those characteristics of a body. By clearly discerning these characteristics that God lacks, one's distinguishes God from all other beings and gains a clearer sense of His uniqueness and oneness. The Rav states:

> On the one hand, Maimonides designated the knowledge of the Creator as the guiding criteria for man, as his ultimate end. On the other hand, Maimonides held the view that knowledge of God is not in the realm of human cognition. Are there two greater opposites then these? The substance of his answer is that negative cognition does not forfeit its status as cognition…The negative theology constitutes the great ideal of *homo religiosus*; it is the "telos" of his noetic process (which will never and can never be entirely realized) and the "end point" of his knowledge-the cognition of the riddle without end (negative cognition) through affirmative cognition. It is for the purpose of unending realization of this idea that *homo religiosus* has been commanded to engage profoundly in rendering an account of the world, to occupy himself with the "natural science" and the "divine science" and this cognition is entirely affirmative and not negative. To be sure, negation is always distantly visible as the goal and final aim of knowledge; however, the process of cognition itself from its "beginning" until its "end" takes on shape in a whirl of colors against an affirmative backdrop. Negation is only the actualization of the cognitive process and the realization of the act of affirmative cognition in its fullness. (HM, p. 11-12)

To be clear, Rabbi Soloveitchik does not see the true *homo religiosus* as a person uninterested or uninvolved in cognition at the deepest level. The difference between cognitive man and *homo religiosus* is not in what they do, but in why they do it. For the cognitive man, the cognitive act is a means to understanding the physical world-to discover its mechanisms and to utilize this knowledge for technology and mastery. Cognition for the cognitive man is a this-worldly activity. The *homo religiosus*, though equally involved in cognitive activities, studies the world for a different purpose. *Homo religiosus* studies the physical world to discern hints and insight about that which is beyond the world–higher realms of being that cannot be cognized, but can be sensed and to which one can be drawn as they are more proximate emanations from God. One only has to read in Maimonides Mishneh Torah, Laws of the Foundations of Torah, to understand the desire of the *homo religiosus*:

> What is the path (to attain) love and fear of Him? When a person contemplates His wondrous and great deeds and creations and appreciates His infinite wisdom that surpasses all comparison, he will immediately love, praise, and glorify (Him), yearning with tremendous desire to know (God's) great name, as David stated: "My soul thirsts for the Lord, for the living God" (Psalms 42:3).

Here Maimonides describes cognition for the sake of sensing something greater that is beyond cognition, as the Rav described the quest of *homo religiosus*. First the person "contemplates His wondrous and great deeds and creations and appreciates His infinite wisdom…". This leads to the sense of wonder and desire for God – "he will immediately love, praise and glorify (Him) yearning with tremendous desire to know (God's) great name…"

Rabbi Soloveitchik bringing Maimonides as the illustration of the *homo religiosus* makes abundantly clear that the *homo religiosus* does not describe the person who dismisses the value or efficacy of cognition altogether. The person who sees the knowledge of the world or of the Creator as being a solely intuitive or emotional activity, void of rigorous cognition is neither a cognitive man nor a *homo religiosus*. The Rav portrays this type of person as a fool at best and an evil person at worst. As we quoted from the essay's footnote # 4, earlier:

> ...the entire Romantic aspiration to escape from the domain of knowledge, the rebellion against the authority of objective, scientific cognition which has found its expression in the biologistic philosophies of Bergson, Nietzsche, Spengler, Klages, and their followers and in the phenomenological, existential, and antiscientific school of Heidegger and his coterie, and from the midst of which there arose in various forms the sanctification of vitality and intuition, the veneration of instinct, the desire for power, the glorification of the emotional-affective life and the flowing, surging stream of subjectivity, the lavishing of extravagant praise on the Faustian type and the Dionysian personality... have brought complete chaos and human depravity to the world....The individual who frees himself from the rational principle and who casts off the yoke of objective thought will in the end turn destructive and lay waste the enter created order. (HM, Note #4, p. 141)

One of main points made by the Rav in Halakhic Man's Part 1, Section 3 is to distinguish the *homo religiosus* from the individual whose chosen path to God sidesteps cognition as an essential requirement. The Rav has no respect for those whose "veneration of instinct, the desire for power, the glorification of the emotional-affective life and the flowing, surging stream of subjectivity" are at the heart of their quest for knowledge, religious or otherwise. The *homo religiosus*, on the other hand, though distinct from the cognitive man and the halakhic man, is a noble individual and a legitimate truth-seeker with a focused desire to cognize for the sake of accessing realms of existence beyond the world of time, space and human culture.

Chapter Four

In this chapter Rabbi Soloveitchik contrasts the two distinct ways of viewing the world employed by *homo religiosus* and cognitive man. It is these differing frames of reference regarding the world around them that is at the heart of their two divergent intellectual objectives. For the *homo religiosus* the world is a phenomenon that exists on multiple levels. This multi-layered existence the Rav terms "ontic pluralism". The lower levels of existence are those we contact with our senses and cognize with our minds. But there exists, for the *homo religiosus* higher, purer levels of being which the person can intuit and connect to, but not via the senses or thought as much as through wonder and longing. The Rav states:

> Ontic pluralism is the very foundation of the world view of homo religiosus. When he approaches the world in order to cognize and evaluate it, he attempts to find in this concrete and physical world the traces of higher worlds, all of which are wholly good and eternal. He seeks to discover the sources of the plenitude in being and of the fullness of the cosmos in supernal ontic realms that are pristine and pure…This transcendent approach to reality constitutes a primary feature of the profile of the man of God. *Homo religiosus* is dissatisfied, unhappy with this world. He searches for an existence that is above empirical reality. This world is a pale image of another world. (HM, p 13)

As we mentioned earlier, Maimonides is presented by the Rav as an example of the *homo religiosus* who studies the physical-temporal existence which is accessible by cognition, and through this gains access to those higher realms which are "immune" to cognition. We are describing here the negative theology which the Rav references in the essay and which we quoted earlier. It is interesting that the Rav does not provide any other specific examples of the *homo religiosus*, either among the Jewish people or among religionists in general. I believe it would be helpful to understand the Rav's *homo religiosus* by drawing upon a number of relevant statements from Rav Chaim of Volozhin's classic text *Nefesh Hachaim*. In Chapter 13 Rav Chaim states:

> In the same way, every word one speaks has an effect on the higher world, as it says, "For behold, He forms mountains and creates winds; He recounts to a person what were the words (he spoke) Amos 4:13). The prophet warns: "Since you live in the lowly physical world, you cannot fathom how each single word you utter has either a constructive or destructive effect on the upper worlds. You may even think: What difference can my insignificant small talk make in the higher worlds? Let me assure you that every trivial word or conversation is stored away and never lost."… The Zohar says: When you discuss Torah thoughts, your words soar on high…giving rise to joy in Heaven and on earth. From every word of Torah or prayer many angels are created. Conversely, harmful talk creates worlds of falsehood and brings about destruction in higher worlds (Nefesh HaChaim – Gate 1, Chapter 13-translated by Avraham Yaakov Finkel).

Rav Chaim Volozhin's statement provides insight into the perspective of *homo religiosus* who holds that what takes place on the earthly plane is meaningful due to its impact on higher realms. Looking at the world through this prism of *"ontic pluralism"* the world of time and space we inhabit loses a certain essential value and its happenings are viewed more as a means to ends that are taking place simultaneously in higher realms of existence. Similarly

Rav Chaim Volozhin states in the same work, *Nefesh HaChaim:*

> As the Zohar explains, just as all spiritual powers above have their counterparts in man, so does each mitzvah correspond to a part of the human body. When a person fulfills a mitzvah with one of his limbs, he causes a spiritual reaction in the higher world that corresponds to that limb, either raising it toward its ultimate destiny or increasing its kedushah....To summarize: Man is the soul of a myriad of worlds. How is this to be understood? Just as every motion of one's limbs is activated by his soul, so are the destinies of the spiritual worlds-their continuance or destruction-determined by the actions of man (in observing or transgressing the mitzvot). (Nefesh HaChaim, Gate 1, Chapter 6).

The motivation and focus of the *homo religoisus* is not fundamentally focused on the bringing of holiness "down" into this world in which we live or in bringing this world to moral or intellectual fruition. As we will see, this is the objective of halakhic man. However for *homo religiosus*, as represented by Rav Chaim Volozhin, the "flow" is reversed, with the performance of *mitzvot* in our world has a perfecting impact on higher worlds that are "repaired" by our good acts down here. Rav Chaim Volozhin explains:

> And when a Jew observes the mitzvos properly, the mitzvos have a beneficial effect on the higher worlds, even if he does not understand their mystical meanings. Each mitzvah generates an upsurge of kedushah and spiritual light, and gives power to G-d. For G-d ordained the nature of the worlds that they should be governed by the deeds of man, and that each mitzvah that is performed on earth should ascend on high, here it accomplishes its designated goal. (Nefesh HaChaim, Gate 1, Chapter 22)

To be clear, the Rabbi Soloveitchik does not cite Rav Chaim Volozhin in the Halakhic Man essay as being an example of the *homo religiosus*. The Rav, would of course have a thorough knowledge of Rav Chaim Volozhin's work *Nefesh HaChaim*. Rav Chaim Volozhin's daughter Rivkah was the mother of the Rav's grandfather, Rav Yosef Dov Soloveitchik (the Beis Halevi). So Rav Chaim Volozhin was the Rav's great, great, great grandfather. Also Rav Chaim Volozhin was the founder of the Yeshiva of Volozhin where the Rav grandfather, Rav Chaim Soloveitchik, served as a senior lecturer and developed the "Brisker Derech" of learning Talmud. The Rav was fully invested in this approach to learning and taught it to thousands of rabbinic students at Yeshiva University in New York City over a 40 year period.

The *Homo Religiosus* in Science and Philosophy

Rabbi Soloveitchik clarifies that the longing of the *homo religiosus* for purer realms beyond the one we physically inhabit is not limited to religious thinkers. In the areas of science and philosophy there have been profound, highly influential *homo religiosus* types. Perhaps the most prominent of all would be Plato, for whom the world of "ideas" was the a higher existence with our inhabited world being a lower shadow form. The Rav bring a long list of pivotal philosophers and religionists who have incorporated these "other worldly" elements into their ontology. They include Aristotle, Philo, Neo-Platonists, Berkley, Spinoza, Kant, Christian and Arab Scholasticism, Husserl and Scheler, and Herman Cohen. Though their approaches vary widely, they all share a common element, as Rabbi Soloveitchik explains:

> ...all constitute traces of religious thought, which yearns for its Creator and rebels against the concrete reality that so entirely surrounds it. A soul overwhelmed by religious longings may, at certain times, stray amid the paths of secular knowledge." (HM, p. 14)

Rabbi Soloveitchik provides a broad definition of *homo religiosus*, including within the category all those who "rebel against the concrete reality that so entirely surrounds us." All those who see a world beyond this one as higher, truer or more fundamental in its nature, would share the *homo religiosus* world view.

Varieties of *Homo Religiosus* and Their Practices

The Rav explains that different varieties of *homo religiosus* take different paths on their quests to accessing these higher realms. Although some may see the most efficient method as being an ascetic lifestyle, others may take what Rabbi Soloveitchik calls a more "life-affirming approach", which I interpret as meaning one that enjoys or even indulges in the pleasures and enjoyment of this world. But as divergent as these paths are, they are unified in their objective of using this world as a means to contact with other and higher worlds. Rabbi Soloveitchik writes:

> Sometimes the craving for transcendence clothes itself in an ascetic garb, in an act of negation of life and of this world, in a denial of the worthwhile nature of existence. The longing of homo religiosus for a supernal world that extends beyond the bounds of concrete reality has been embodied in many

> doctrines of asceticism, renunciation, and self-affliction. At such moments homo religiosus is of the opinion that suffering and torments, fasting and seclusion are the means which convey eternal felicity to man and bring him under the wings of the supernal…At other times this motif may assume an extreme form of affirmation of the world and approval of reality. However, even according to this stance, concrete, empirical reality serves only as a springboard from which man may make his plunge into the supernal, and it is the supernal realm alone that serves as the object of the religious individual's deepest longing, the goal of his ultimate quest. Naturally, between the two extremes of asceticism on the one hand and affirmation of the world on the other, there are a number of intermediate positions that graft together elements from both stances and create hybrid religious and moral systems. (HM, p. 15-16)

The quest of *homo religiosus* to sense and connect with these higher realms of being and to escape his "entrapment" within this world is contrasted by Rav with the decidedly "this-worldly" nature of halakhic man.

Chapter Five

In this chapter Rabbi Soloveitchik begins to portray the unique character of halakhic man. The Rav utilizes his descriptions of cognitive man and *homo religiosus* as his departure point for this portrayal. Halakhic man does incorporate some of the qualities of each, although with his own unique objective and worldview. Unlike *homo religiosus*, although the halakhic man's nature is fully dedicated to the service of God, he does not seek or interest himself with accessing higher spiritual realms which *homo religiosus* sees as essential and irresistible in searching for holiness and God. The Rav states:

> Halakhic man's approach to reality is, at the outset, devoid of any element of transcendence. (HM, p. 17)

In addition, although halakhic man is a highly analytic and logical thinker, he is not focused on understanding the workings of the physical world for the benefit of improving the quality of human life or to satisfy his intellectual curiosity. As Rabbi Soloveitchik explains:

> Halakhic man studies reality not because he is motivated by plain curiosity the way theoretical man is; nor is he driven to explore the world by any fear of being or anxiety of nonbeing. (HM, p. 17)

So what is the halakhic man's interest in studying and analyzing the world around him? What is the nature of what the Rav calls halakhic man's "cognitive-normative" approach? It is at this point that the Rav takes a definitive step in the essay. He explains that halakhic man comes to all his cognition with a unique set a logical categories through which he sees the world. Borrowing from the philosopher Emanuel Kant's formulation that human being don't see the world as it actually is, but through the filter of logical categories that are inherent to the human mind, Rabbi Soloveitchik explains that the halakhic man sees the world filtered through the categories of Jewish law – the Halakhah-which he has learned with great clarity and completeness and which encompasses every situation that any person may encounter in life from the most ordinary to the most dramatic. It is with this unique categorical perspective that halakhic man merges the system of halakhah with the physical world he encounters. This results in halakhic man's viewing of the world and human culture as the process of realizing the abstract halakhic system of law and obligations in the concrete world we live each day. Rabbi Soloveitchik writes:

> Halakhic man orients himself to reality through a priori images of the world which he bears in the deep recesses of his personality. We may, if we so desire, call this a cognitive-normative approach, but it is not to be identified with the cognitive and ethical orientation of which the philosophers, the cognitive men par excellence speak. (HM, p. 17)

Cognitive Man's Dual Relationship with Reality

Rabbi Soloveitchik's essay provides something of a primer on philosophy in his attempt to place halakhic man within the scheme of other approaches to reality. He explains the major divergence of cognitive man's two approaches to reality as "(1) an empirical, a posteriori approach; (2) an a priori approach." The Rav writes:

We know that cognitive man has a dual relationship with reality: (1) an empirical, a posteriori approach; (2) an apriori approach. And it need not be emphasized that the entire dispute between rationalists and empiricists centers around this problem. In truth this disagreement symbolizes two different directions in man's relationship to reality..." (HM, p.18)

At this point the Rav describes the basic approach of the empiricist type of cognitive man whose seeks knowledge of the world through the senses. He searches for patterns in the data and from this constructs theories and structures to explain these patterns. The Rav states regarding the empiricist subset of cognitive man as follows:

Cognitive man, in this instance, approaches the world without preconceived programs, without any elaborate preparations. He gropes in the darkness, is astonished and amazed by the plethora of phenomena and by the "chaos and void" which prevails in the realm of reality, until he stumbles across a repetition of events in a certain order, which he had dimly sensed to begin with, as a result of which he can construct rules and establish laws that can serve as a beacon illuminating the road on which he travels through the cosmos. (HM, p. 18)

The 17th century British philosopher John Locke explained in "An Essay on Human Understanding" that the only knowledge human can have is *a posteriori* (based on experience) as opposed to the apriori (prior to experience) that is so central to the cognitive rationalist. He portrayed the human mind as a "blank slate" (*table rasa*) "white paper" on which the experiences one has through the senses are recorded. In empiricism, ideas are formed by reflection on perceptions and formulations the mind creates from these perceptions. For the cognitive empiricist there exist no pre-existing eternal ideas through which a person perceives and understands the world. Ideas come into existence only after perception. As we will see this is distinct from the cognitive rationalist who believes that ideas are inherent and exist prior to experience and determine the nature of our perceptions and how we experience the world.

At the other end of the cognitive spectrum is the rationalist cognitive type who, as we will see, in many ways resembles the *a priori* approach of the halakhic man. For the cognitive rationalist the exterior world is neither the object of his investigation nor the actual source of his knowledge. For the rationalist, there are categories and concepts that are present in the mind before experiencing the outside world (i.e., *a priori*) and his work is to clarify and purify his understanding of this inborn knowledge. There is some degree of correlation between the physical world observed and the abstract world that the rationalist constructs. But understanding the exterior world around him is not his fundamental objective. Rabbi Soloveitchik writes:

> In order to overcome the mystery in existence, he constructs an ideal, ordered and fixed world, one that is perfectly clear and lucid; he fashions an a priori, ideal creation with which he is greatly pleased. This creation does not cause him any anxiety. It does not attempt to elude him; it cannot conceal knowledge. Whenever he wishes to orient himself to reality and to superimpose his a priori ideal system upon the realm of concrete empirical existence, he comes with his teachings in hand-his a priori teaching. He has no wish to passively cognize reality as it is in itself. Rather, first he creates the ideal a priori image, the ideal structure, and then compares it

with the real world...More, even when the theoretician with his a priori system gets involved in the technological, utilitarian aspects of science, there, too, his sole aim is to reveal the parallelism that prevails between the ideal series and the concrete series. (HM, p. 18)

Perhaps the most famous modern day example from physics of this focus on the theoretical over the concrete parallel occurred when Albert Einstein's Theory of General Relativity was being put to the test in 1919 by Sir Arthur Eddington. This attempt to find empirical confirmation of the theory was through the observation of light deflection, noting the change in position of stars as they passed near the Sun in the celestial sphere. The observations were performed by Arthur Eddington and his collaborators during the total solar eclipse of May 29, 1919, when the stars near the Sun (at that time in the constellation Taurus) could be observed due to the darkness near the Sun observable during this phenomenon. Observations were made simultaneously in the cities of Sobral, Ceará, Brazil and in São Tomé and Príncipe on the west coast of Africa. Einstein's theory was confirmed by these observations and was published on the front page of most major newspapers throughout the world. It made Einstein and his Theory of General Relativity world-famous. When asked by his assistant what his reaction would have been if the observations had not been confirmed by Eddington and Dyson in 1919, Einstein famously quipped: "Then I would feel sorry for the dear Lord. The theory is correct anyway." Although this outrageous statement of Einstein was meant to be humorous, and has a somewhat blasphemous tinge to it, it is worth reflecting on it in order to better understand the point the Rav is making about the cognitive realist's worldview.

What did Einstein mean when he said "the theory is correct anyway"? This strange statement reflects the belief by those most sensitive and capable of assessing the quality of mathematical formulations, that their beauty and elegance is an indication of their convergence with the underlying structure of the physical world. Regarding this correlation Einstein stated:

> Our experience up to date justifies us in feeling sure that in Nature is actualized the ideal of mathematical simplicity. It is my conviction that pure mathematical construction enables us to discover the concepts and the laws connecting them, which gives us the key to understanding nature... In a certain sense, therefore, I hold it true that pure thought can grasp reality, as the ancients dreamed. (In Herbert Spencer Lecture at Oxford (10 Jun 1933), 'On the Methods of Theoretical Physics'. Printed in *Discovery* (Jul 1933), 14, 227

Although it is difficult for non-mathematicians to understand the idea of a mathematical formulation being "beautiful" or "elegant", this is a strongly held position by leaders in the fields of mathematics and physics. Einstein commented on this phenomenon:

> One seeks the most general ideas of operation which will bring together in simple, logical and unified form the largest possible circle of formal relationships. In this effort toward logical beauty spiritual formulas are discovered necessary for the deeper penetration into the laws of nature. (In letter (1 May 1935), Letters to the Editor, 'The Late Emmy Noether: Professor Einstein Writes in Appreciation of a Fellow-Mathematician', *New York Times* (4 May 1935), 12.)

Paul Dirac, one of the leading physicists of the 20th century, whose text "*The Principles of Quantum Mechanics*, published in 1930, is a landmark in the history of science. It quickly became one of the standard textbooks on the subject and is still used today. Dirac wrote in a 1963 Scientific American article:

> If this theory is really beautiful, then it necessarily will appear as a fine model of important physical phenomena. It is necessary to search for these phenomena to develop applications of the beautiful mathematical theory and to interpret them as predictions of new laws of physics. It is more important to have beauty in one's equations than to have them fit experiment. It seems that if one is working from the point of view of getting beauty in one's equations, and if one has really a sound insight, one is on a sure line of progress.

This astounding idea, widely held by mathematicians and physicists is that a sensing of the beauty of a human mathematical formulation is an indicator of its truthfulness and accuracy in correlating with the physical universe of time, space and matter. This "faith" has often been supported by developments in the physical sciences. So perhaps Einstein's strange statement that even if Eddington's experiment did not confirm the General Theory of Relativity that "it is correct anyway" was a belief by Einstein that the elegance and beauty of the equation was so great that his faith in its correlation with the physical world "overruled" the results of any particular experimental test.

Returning the Rabbi Soloveitchik's profile of cognitive man in the "Halakhic Man" essay, he draws on mathematics as the area of study to distinguish between the cognitive rationalist and the cognitive empiricist. In the notes at the conclusion of "Halakhic Man" the Rav states:

> When epistemological doctrine speaks of the a priori nature of mathematics, it is not approaching the subject from a psychogenetic vantage point but rather from the perspective of a systematic, transcendental outlook concerning the non-temporal nature of mathematical knowledge and its inherent necessity and truth. This approach is particularly exemplified by the transcendental method of Kant as interpreted by the philosophy of Hermann Cohen. (HM, Note 24, p. 147)

The Rav clarifies in this note that mathematics is viewed by the cognitive rationalists transcendentally and not just as a skill resulting from the physical nature of the human brain ("not from a psychogenetic vantage point"). It is transcendental in that mathematical insight results from contact with a higher realm of existence, similar to Plato's eternally existing Ideas. Thus the Rav's language in the note–"the non-temporal nature of mathematics and its inherent necessity and truth." From this vantage point the greatness of a mathematical formulation can be sensed inherently due to its structure and elegance. The correlation of the mathematical formula with external phenomena is important but not the only indication of the "correctness" of the mathematical formula.

To some degree the cognitive rationalists apply the poet Jonathan Keats' most famous verse to mathematics. As the poet wrote in "Ode to a Grecian Urn" –"Beauty is truth, truth beauty-that is all Ye know on earth, and all ye need to know." Along these lines, Einstein responded when asked about the possibility that his mathematical formulation of the General Theory of Relativity did not correlate with the observed measurements of Eddington that "the theory is correct anyway". Perhaps Einstein meant by his statement that from the point of view of its beauty, elegance and completeness there is a "correctness" to the mathematics of the theory and that must be correct and that eventually measurement would confirm its correlation with the physical world.

I will conclude this section with a brief excerpt from the Stanford Encyclopedia of Philosophy entry titled "Rationalism vs. Empiricism":

> The dispute between rationalism and empiricism concerns the extent to which we are dependent upon sense experience in our effort to gain knowledge. Rationalists claim that there are significant ways in which our concepts and knowledge are gained independently of sense experience. Empiricists claim that sense experience is the ultimate source of all our concepts and knowledge.
> (https://plato.stanford.edu/entries/rationalism-empiricism/)

In the next chapter we will see that Rabbi Soloveitchik draws on the profile of the cognitive rationalist in his depiction of halakhic man.

Chapter 6

In this chapter Rabbi Soloveitchik provides the first detailed profile of halakhic man. The previous descriptions of cognitive man and *homo religiosus* were provided to orient the reader to the unique features of halakhic man who, we will see, possesses characteristics of both. The Rav begins his outline in applying certain elements of the cognitive man (specifically the cognitive rationalist) to halakhic man. Specifically, just as the cognitive rationalist approaches the world with the apriori truths of his ideal, abstract mathematical and logical systems, and then views phenomena through these lenses, so too the halakhic man comes to the world with his ideal halakhic system of Jewish law and sees the world of phenomena through the categories that it provides.

> When halakhic man approaches reality, he comes with his Torah, given to him from Sinai, in hand. He orients himself to the worlds by means of fixed statutes and firm principles. An entire corpus of precepts and laws guides his along the path leading to existence. Halakhic man, well furnished with rules, judgments, and fundamental principles, draws near the world with an a priori relation. His approach begins with an ideal creation and concludes with a real one. To whom may he be compared? To a mathematician who fashions an ideal world and then uses it for the purpose of establishing a relationship between it and the real world, as was explained above. (HM, p. 19)

Although the Rav makes clear here that the Halakhah "was received from God", he continues to focus on the parallel between the cognitive rationalist and halakhic man. Just as physicist believe that all physical phenomena in the world are understandable through the prism of mathematics, so too halakhic man understands that all the world's phenomena can be categorized and analyzed through the halakhic system. Rabbi Soloveitchik states: "There is no phenomenon, entity, or object in this concrete world which the a priori Halakhah does not approach with its ideal standard." (HM, p.19)

The Rav continues with the well-known description of a water spring and how this physical entity is perceived and analyzed by halakhic man, not primarily through the laws of scientific categories and mathematical formula, but instead through the equally precise, all-encompassing and specific categories of halakhic law. He writes:

> When halakhic man comes across a spring bubbling quietly, he already possesses a fixed, a priori relationship with this real phenomenon: the complex of laws regarding the halakhic construct of a spring. The spring is fit for the immersion of a *zav* (a man with a discharge); it may serve as *mei hatat* (waters of expiation); it purifies with flowing water; it does not require a fixed quantity of forty se'ahs; etc. (See Maimonides, *Laws of Immersion Pools*, 9:8) When halakhic man approaches a real spring, he gazes at it and carefully examines its nature. He possesses, a priori, ideal principles and precepts which establish the character of the spring as a halakhic construct, and he uses the statutes for a purpose of determining normative law; does the real spring correspond to the requirements of the ideal Halakhah or not?

So, just as the rational cognitive man applies the abstract, pristine laws of geometry to understand the actual shape of a planet's orbit, similarly the halakhic man utilizes the precise abstract categories of halakhic law to understand and act upon the actual physical world he perceives, analyzes and defines. His intellectual goal is to find correlation and convergence between the abstract, pure halakhah and the specific aspect of the physical world he perceives. The Rav brings another case which seems to me to express that even the intense beauty and grandeur that one might experience through observing a glorious sunset or sunrise is subsumed into the halakhic man's perspective of seeing all phenomena through the halakhic lens. Rabbi Soloveitchik continues:

> When halakhic man looks to the western horizon and sees the fading rays of the setting sun or to the eastern horizon and sees the first light of dawn and the glowing rays of the rising sun, he knows that this sunset or sunrise imposes upon him anew obligations and commandments... The sunset on Sabbath and holiday eves sanctifies the day: the profane and the holy are dependent upon a natural cosmic phenomenon- the sun sinking below the horizon. It is not anything transcendent that creates holiness but rather the visible reality-the regular cycle of the natural order... He approaches existential space with an a priori yardstick, with fixed laws and principles, precepts that were revealed to Moses on Mount Sinai...He perceives space by means of these laws just like the mathematician who gazes at existential space by means of the ideal geometric space. (HM, p. 22)

The Rav is portraying a pure type, the halakhic man, whose entire being and personality is dedicated to this pursuit of halakhic study and clarification, with the application of this system to the world around him. This is why the term "halakhic" is an adjective modifying the term "man" in the term "halakhic man". The Halakhah completely defines the personality and nature of this type of man. He is not simply a person who applies or follows the halakhic system. The Halakhah becomes so much a part of the person that it governs how he sees everything around him and becomes the primary categories of mind with which he perceives and interacts with the world. It is for this reason that we will see that the "halakhic man" is a man of this world and not the next one. The halakhah applies in this world (*olam hazeh*), but not, according to the Rav in the world to come after death. Both study and application of the halakhah is a human activity carried out while man is alive. So since halakhic man is fully committed and absorbed in this halakhic process, why would he concern himself or long for the world to come?

The Breadth of Halakhic Application

Rabbi Soloveitchik describes the all-encompassing nature of the halakhic system and that all phenomena are under its domain. He writes:

> There is no real phenomenon to which halakhic man does not possess a fixed relationship from the outset and a clear, definitive, a priori orientation. The Halakhah encompasses laws of business, torts, neighbors, plaintiff and defendant, creditor and debtor, partners, agents, workers, artisans, bailees, etc. Family life-marriage, divorce, *halitzah, sotah,* conjugal refusal (*mi'in*) the respective rights, obligations, and duties of a husband and a wife-is clarified and elucidated by it. War, the high court, courts and the penalties they impose- all are just a few of the multitude of halakhic subjects....Halakhah has a fixed a priori relationship to the whole of reality in all of its fine and detailed particulars. (HM, p. 22-23)

Interesting, although all things of this world are covered by the Halakhah, not all areas of Halakhah necessarily have an actual counterpart. The Rav explains that these few cases where the halakhah remains in the abstract without an actual corollary in the real world, do not cause any particular dismay for the halakhic man. He writes:

> And when many halakhic concepts do not correspond with the phenomena of the real world, halakhic man is not at all distressed. His deepest desire is not the realization of the Halakhah but rather the ideal construction which was given to him from Sinai, and this ideal construction exists forever. "There never was an idolatrous city and there never will be. For what purpose, then was its law written? Expound it and receive reward! There never was a leprous house and never will be. For what purpose then, was its law written. Expound it and receive a reward! There never was a rebellious son and never will be. For what purpose, then, was his law written? Expound it and receive reward." (HM, p. 23)

The Halakhic man is concerned with the world and the application of the abstract halakhah to the actual situations he encounters or studies. But, the Rav makes clear, this is not his ultimate interest. At the core is the halakhah for its own sake and the halakhic man seeks to understand its meaning and depth and hold the system within his mind with complete clarity and understanding. This objective is not deterred or diminished simply because certain cases of the Halakhah do not and will never take place in the material world.

The theoretic Halakhah, not the practical decision, the ideal creation, not the empirical one, represent the longing of halakhic man. Here we meet for the first time in the essay, Rabbi Soloveitchik's grandfather, Rabbi Hayyim Soloveitchik who is portrayed many times throughout the essay as an halakhic man *par excellence*.

Rabbi Hayyim Soloveitchik (1853-1918), was a rabbinic leader and Talmudic scholar credited as the founder of the extremely popular Brisker approach to Talmudic study within Judaism. He was born in Volozhin, where his father, Rabbi Yosef Dov Soloveitchik served as a lecturer in the famous Volozhiner Yeshiva. After a few years, his father was appointed as a Rav in Slutzk, where young Chaim was first educated. While still a youngster, his genius and lightning-quick grasp were widely recognized. Eventually, following many years as a senior lecturer in the renowned Volozhiner Yeshiva, he accepted a position as Rav of Brest, Belarus (*Brisk* in Yiddish).

He is a member of the Soloveitchik-family rabbinical dynasty and is commonly known as *Reb Chaim Brisker* ("Rabbi Chaim [from] Brisk"). He is considered the founder of the "Brisker method" (in Yiddish: *Brisker Derech*), a method of highly exacting and analytical Talmudic study that focuses on precise definitions and categorizations of Jewish law as commanded in the Torah with particular emphasis on the legal writings of Maimonides. He had two famous sons, Rabbi Yitzchak Zev Soloveitchik (also known as Rabbi Velvel Soloveitchik or the Brisker Rav) who subsequently moved to Israel and Rabbi Moshe Soloveitchik who moved to the United States and subsequently served as the *Rosh Yeshiva* of Yeshiva Yitzchak Elchanan in New York (Yeshiva University) and who was succeeded by his own son Rabbi Joseph B. Soloveitchik. (https://en.wikipedia.org/wiki/Chaim_Soloveitchik)

In the essay's first citing of Rabbi Hayyim Soloveitchik, it is to describe his inclusion of those parts of the Talmudic law in the curriculum of the Yeshiva Volozhin which he taught in their entirety, although they were not practiced at that time and are still not actually performed, due to the destruction of the Temple in Jerusalem over two thousand years ago. Yeshiva Volozhin's learning of those parts which are not currently practiced is brought by the Rav as evidence of the primacy of the abstract Halakhah over the applied, functioning Halakhah in the mind and values of the halakhic man. Rabbi Soloveitchik writes:

> The Yeshiva of Volozhin introduced the study of the entire Talmud from beginning to end-from Berakhot to Niddah-in place of the previous practice of skipping over those tractates which do not deal with laws that are practiced nowadays. R. Hayyim Soloveitchik, aside from his regular lecture at the yeshiva of Volozhin, would also deliver a parallel lecture on the tractates Zevahim (animal offerings) and Menahot (meal offering)... This stance has been a fundamental characteristic of halakhists from time immemorial. (HM, p. 24-25)

Rabbi Soloveitchik also refers to perhaps the greatest expression of this placing of the abstract system before the system that is actually operating at the time. This is Maimonides' (the Rambam's) work the *Mishneh Torah (Yad Ha-Hazakah)* which codified the entire corpus of the halakhic system making no distinction between those parts of the halakhah that are currently operating and those that have been "on hold" since the destruction of the Second Temple, which occurred over one thousand years prior to Maimonides' completion of the Mishneh Torah. The Rav states:

> Maimonides in his great code of law, *Yad Ha-Hazakah*, codified all of the laws of the Torah from the first mishnah in Berakhot to the last mishnah in Uktzin...Maimonides describes the order of events on the fifteenth night of Nisan,

he "forgets" temporarily that he is living approximately one thousand years after the destruction of the Temple and paints the image of the service of the holy festival night in a wealth of colors that dazzle the eye, that reflects the Passover service as it was celebrated thousands of years ago in ancient Jerusalem and as it once again will be celebrated in the era of the Messiah…The seder with which Maimonides is dealing is an ideal conception of Passover night. (HM, excerpts from p. 25-28).

The Rav has presented a dual-dimension to the personality of halakhic man. On the one hand his core ideal is the study and understanding of the abstract halakhic system. This he endeavors to master in its entirety, regardless of its actualization in the real world. Just as the theoretical mathematician is focused on his abstract system, without concern as to whether there is a correlate to which it applies in the world of time and space. The Rav writes:

> Such is also the way of the mathematician! When Riemann and Lobachevski discovered the possibility of a non-Euclidean space, they did not pay any attention to the existential space in which we all live and which is Euclidean from beginning to end. They were concerned with an ideal mathematical construction, and in that ideal world they discerned certain features of a geometric space different from ours. Afterwards, physicist such as Einstein and his circle appeared, and they utilized the concept of a non-Euclidean space in order to explain certain physical phenomena. The ideal-geometric space found its actualization in the real world. (HM, p. 29)

But the halakhic man is not without his desire to actualize this abstract halakhah in the real world. There is an additional part of his dedication to God and the halakhic system He has revealed, to actualize it in human civilization. As we will see this desire to "bring holiness down from the heavens to earth" is a secondary but strongly held objective of halakhic man and one that he pursues with great determination.

Chapter Seven

We now come to one of the central ideas of the essay. Perhaps the defining concept of "Halakhic Man" is Rabbi Soloveitchik's characterization of him as being focused on earthly life and not on the next world or higher realms of existence beyond the one we live day to day. Halakhic man is decidedly "this-worldly" and is not particularly interested in that which is beyond this earthly realm. In this aspect he is the polar opposite of the *homo religiosus* whose objective is to transcend the boundaries of this world and reach for higher, purer realms of existence, whether during life or after death. The Rav writes:

> Halakhic man does not long for a transcendent world, for "supernal" levels of a pure, pristine existence, for was not the ideal world, halakhic man's deepest desire, his darling child-created only for the purpose of being actualized in our real world? It is this world which constitutes the stage for the Halakhah, the setting for halakhic man's life. It is here that the Halakhah can be implemented to a greater or lesser degree. "Better is one hour of Torah and *mitzvot* in this world than the whole life of the world to come," stated the tanna in Avot (4:17), and this declaration is the watchword of the halakhist. (HM, p. 30)

Halakhic man is a unique amalgam. He is wholly God-centered, as the Halakhah is for him the revelation of God's will to man and the defining core of his mission and his identity. He is also a fervent servant of God in his complete dedication to fulfilling and actualizing the Halakhah. But, at the same time, he is decidedly focused on this world and not the next. His purpose isn't to know God per se or to uncover the secrets of higher realms of being. For halakhic man, the system of Halakhah is his royal road to approaching God in this earthly life and serving his Creator in his day-to-day activities. This is, so to speak, his soul's sole concern. How distinct and distant he is from his God-centered counterpart, the *homo religiosus*, who as the Rav stated earlier, "is dissatisfied, unhappy with this world. *Homo religiosus* searches for an existence that is above empirical reality. This world is a pale image of another world." (HM, p. 13)

I believe that one of the main objectives of Rabbi Soloveitchik's essay is to dispel the idea that the Halakhic man lacks a fully developed spiritual life or is in some way deficient in his love and dedication to God or his belief in the reward of the world to come. The Rav notes this misunderstanding of the halakhic man by the *homo religiosus*. He states:

> Not only will the universal *homo religiosus* not understand this statement, but he will have only contempt for, as if, heaven forbid, it is intended to deny the pure and exalted life after death. (HM, p. 30).

Who is this "universal *homo religiosus*", the Rav speaks of? Could it be the Christian believer who sees this world as "a vale of tears" and awaits the holiness and sweetness of heaven? Could it be the Jewish mystic or Chasid or longs to merge with God and leave this earthly world of separation and illusion behind? Rabbi Soloveitchik does not explain. But whoever looks at the humble, devout Jew, totally occupied with the seemingly endless minutia of following every detail of halakhah in even the seemingly most mundane of activities, and does not see a greatness and a deep holiness – the Rav is emphatically informing that person that they are in error. This appearance of hyper-focus on "small details of small things" is spiritual greatness in disguise. As the Rav will describe later in the essay, the intense and unflagging observance of the Halakhah in all its detail is man's way of bringing holiness into this world and redeeming it. This is a task of great importance and one that the halakhic man recognizes as such. The Rav seeks to dispel the false idea that the casual or uninformed observer might have of these noble individuals, mistakenly viewing them as acting in an automatic, non-reflective manner simply carrying out commands without reflection or a larger perspective.

Halakhic Man's Perspective on Death

Rabbi Soloveitchik explains that the halakhic man's focus on bringing holiness into the world of the living is reflected in his negative outlook towards death. The Rav explains that belief in the next world as one of bliss and great reward is one of the fundamental beliefs of Judaism. However, this being said, the next world and its purity and perfection is a distinct existence from the human one, and one that the halakhic man does not focus on or view as a particular objective or aspiration. Life is viewed by him as precious and death reviled.

> Judaism has a negative attitude toward death: a corpse defiles; a grave defiles; a person who has been defiled by a corpse: (HM, p. 31)

The Rav quotes from the Mishnah: "Better is one hour of Torah and *mitzvot* in this world than the whole life of the world to come". (Avot: 4:17). How is it better? While the life of the world to come is one of bliss and joy, basking in the presence of God. The life in this world is one in which the individual can actively and freely endeavor to change himself and the world and utilize his creativity and will to bring holiness into the world with his thoughts and actions. This is unique to this world and, in this way, exceeds, in this way, the greatness of the life of the world to come. A bit later in the essay the Rav expounds on this idea:

> The Halakhah is not at all concerned with a transcendent world. The world to come is a tranquil, quiet world that is wholly good, wholly everlasting, and wholly eternal, wherein a man will receive the reward for the commandments which he performed in this world. However, the receiving of reward is not a religious act; therefore, halakhic man prefers the real world to a transcendent existence because here, in this world, man is given the opportunity to create, act, accomplish, while there, in the world to come, he is powerless to change anything at all. (HM, p. 32)

The Rav cites a well-known story about the Vilna Gaon, (Rabbi Eliyahu of Vilna-1720-1797) who is considered by many to be the greatest Torah scholar of modern times. The story explains how the Vilna Gaon joyously gave up a portion his reward in the next world to bring holiness in this world. The Rav writes:

> And when a Polish woman of noble birth proved stubborn and demanded, as the purchase price for the fresh, green moist myrtles that grew in her garden, the reward that was reserved for the Gaon for the performance of the commandment, he gladly and wholeheartedly fulfilled her request and "transferred" to her the reward for the commandment of taking the four species. (HM, p. 30)

The Rav explains that the Vilna Gaon joyously sacrificed a portion of his reward in the next world for the opportunity to fulfill a mitzvah in this world with a particular perfection. He writes:

> On that Sukkot, so the folk legend relates, he was exceedingly joyful and told his students: "All my life I grieved, when would I have the opportunity of fulfilling a commandment without receiving a reward, in order that I might thereby fulfill the injunction of Antigonos of Socho: 'Be like the servants who minister to their master without the intent of receiving a reward' (Avot 1:31) and now that I have this opportunity should I not fulfill this commandment with gladness and joy?" (HM, p. 30-31)

The viewing of death in this negative way, Rabbi Soloveitchik explains, is not common to all religions. Many see death as a desirable step in the path towards drawing close to God and as such, celebrate it in different ways. The Rav writes:

> Many religions view the phenomenon of death as a positive spectacle, inasmuch as it highlights and sensitizes the religious consciousness and "sensibility". They, therefore, sanctify death and the grave because it is here that we find ourselves at the threshold of transcendence, at the portal of the world to come. Death is seen as a window filled with light, open to an exalted, supernal realm. Judaism, however, proclaims that coming in contact with the dead precipitates defilement. Judaism abhors death, organic decay and dissolution. It bids one to choose life and sanctify it. Authentic Judaism as reflected in halakhic thought sees in death a terrifying contradiction to the whole of religious life. Death negates the entire magnificent experience of halakhic man. (HM, p. 31)

The personality of halakhic man and the Halakhah merge in this issue of life and death. The position of the Halakhah on an issue becomes part of the persona of the halakhic man. Just as the Halakhah categorizes death as defiling and a phenomenon that results in a restriction from serving God, (one who comes in contact with the dead is restricted from various aspects of participating in Sanctuary or Temple activities), so too the halakhic man has a deeply negative perspective of death which manifests itself emotionally as well as intellectually.

The Torah is For Man, Not Angels

The Rav draws on an intriguing narrative from the Talmud (Shabbat 88b-89a) in which God asks Moses to respond to the angels' "complaints" that the Torah is far too holy and exalted for giving to imperfect human beings: "They (the angels) said to Him (God), "That secret treasure…Thou desirest to give to flesh and blood!" When God said to Moses to answer them, he explains that the Torah, despite its exalted holiness and perfection, is nonetheless made for the struggling, sinning and limiting creation known as the human being. Moses responds:

> Sovereign of the universe! The Torah which Thou givest me, what is written therein? *I am the Lord Thy God, who brought thee out of the land of Egypt* (Exod. 20: 2).' Said he to them (the angels), 'Did you go down to Egypt? Were you enslaved to Pharaoh?, etc. Again what is written therein? *Remember the Sabbath day, to keep it holy* (Exod. 20:8). Do you then perform work that you need to rest?, etc. Again what is written therein? *Honor thy father and thy mother* (Exod. 20:12). Do you have any fathers and mothers? Again, what is written therein? *Thou shalt not murder. Thou shalt not commit adultery. Thou shalt not steal* (Exod. 20:13). Is there jealousy among you; is the Evil Tempter among you?' Straight away they conceded to Him," etc., etc. (HM, p. 33)

Rabbi Soloveitchik explains that this confrontation between Moses and the angels expresses the profoundly earthly character of the Torah and its system of halakhah. He writes:

> The earth and bodily life are the very ground of the halakhic reality. Only against the concrete, empirical backdrop of this world can the Torah be implemented; angels, who neither eat nor drink, who neither quarrel with one another nor are envious of one another are not worthy and fit for the receiving of the Torah. (HM, p. 34)

The Paramount Value of Life in Halakhah

Rabbi Soloveitchik clarifies that the human life is of paramount value in the halakhic system. Human life does not obtain its status within in the system of halakhah due to its role in preparing us for the next world, as it is assessed by Christianity, Islam and those who formulate Judaism as being primarily a preparation for the life of the world to come. This clarification I believe is a core objective of the Rav's essay. The halakhah and Judaism are religiously unique in this regard. This distinction between the value of life as a means to the next life versus the valuing of life for its own sake is fundamental for validating the absolute value of justice and mercy in this world. The Rav will clarify at a number of places in the essay that the "other-worldly" focus of religious value is the cause of much evil and misery carried out in the name of religion. Rabbi Soloveitchik writes:

> The teachings of the Torah do not oppose the laws of life and reality, for were they to clash with this world and were they to negate the value of concrete, physiological-biological existence, then they would contain not mercy,

lovingkindness, and peace but vengeance and wrath. Even if there is only a doubtful possibility that a person's life is in danger, one renders a lenient decision; and as long as one is able to discover some possible danger to life, one may use that doubt to render a lenient decision...This law that *pikuah nefesh*, savings a life, overrides all the commandments and its far-reaching effects are indicative of the high value which the halakhic viewpoint attributes to one's earthly life-indeed they serve to confirm and nurture that value. Temporal life becomes transformed into eternal life; it becomes sanctified and elevated with eternal holiness. (HM, p. 34)

Rabbi Soloveitchik provides a poignant example of how halakhic men have actualized the life-affirming dimension of halakhah in their role as rabbinic leaders and in their personal lives:

My grandfather, R. Hayyim of Brisk, disagreed with the legal view that on the Day of Atonement one feeds a sick person who is in danger (of dying) small amounts of food at a time, each amount less than the forbidden measure of food for that day. Rather he instructed those who were taking care of a sick individual to serve him a regular meal, just as they would on other days. When my father was about to travel to Rasseyn, a town close to Kovno, to take up a rabbinical post, R. Hayyim took him aside and said, "I command you to follow my view regarding a sick person in danger on the Day of Atonement for it is an absolute halakhic truth." (HM, p. 35).

The Rav also explains that it is a tradition among great halakhic men not to visit cemeteries:

The Gaon of Vilna, R. Joseph Dov Soloveitchik, him son, R. Hayyim, his grandson, R. Moses, R. Elijah Pruzna (Feinstein) never visited cemeteries and never prostrated themselves upon the graves of their ancestors. The memory of death would have distracted them from their intensive efforts to study the Torah.

There are many Jewish groups, particularly among the Hasidim, that focus significantly on visiting the graves of great scholars and rebbeim. Most prominent perhaps is the international trips by which thousands come to visit the grave in Uman, Ukraine of Rav Nachman, the founder of the Breslev branch of Hasidim, as well as that of the late Lubavitcher Rebbe, Rav Menachem Schneerson. Whether this centrality of visiting of the graves reflects a more "other-worldly" focus by these Jewish groups is beyond the scope of this analysis, but worthy of reflection in light of the Rav's stating of the opposite tradition being the case among the great halakhic men he mentions.

Halakhic Man's Fear of Death

The most powerful and perhaps surprising example of halakhic man's sense of revulsion towards death that Rabbi Soloveitchik brings for our consideration is another story about his grandfather, Rav Hayyim of Brisk. He writes:

> It is only against this background that we can comprehend a peculiar feature in the character of many great Jewish scholars and halakhic giants: the fear of death. Halakhic man is afraid of death; the dread of dissolution often times seizes hold of him. My uncle, R. Meir Berlin (Bar-Ilan), related the following incident to me. Once he and R. Hayyim of Brisk happened to be staying in the same hotel in Libau on the shore of the Baltic. One fine, clear morning he rose at sunrise and went out on the balcony there to find R. Hayyim sitting- his head between his hands, his glance fixed upon the rays of the rising sun, entirely absorbed in the aesthetic experience of

such a glorious cosmic spectacle and, at the same time, entirely bent beneath the oppressive weight of a soul-shattering melancholy and a black despair. R.Berlin took hold of R. Hayyim's shoulder and shook it: "Why are you so troubled and disturbed, my master and teacher? Is something in particular responsible for your distress?" "Yes," replied R. Hayyim, "I am reflecting upon the end of very man-death."...The halakhic man who gazed at the first rays of the sun and reflected upon the beauty of the world and the nothingness of man in an ecstatic mood of joy intermixed with tragedy is a this-worldly man, an individual given over to concrete reality, who communicates with his Creator, not beyond the bounds of finitude, not in a holy, transcendent realm enwrapped in mystery, but rather in the very midst of the world and the fullness thereof. (HM, p. 36-37).

In relating this incident, the Rav also makes clear that R. Hayyim, though a man focused with his whole being on the meticulous fulfillment of every detail of Jewish law was, simultaneously, a person of great sensitivity and depth, with a profundity that many would not attribute to the Talmud scholar, who the uninformed might mistakenly view as highly unreflective or shallow in nature.

The Transformation of the Mind and Personality by the Halakhah

Rabbi Soloveitchik explains that for those who fully embrace the study and practice of halakhah, the system of ideas and imperatives has the power to fundamentally transform the mind and personality. As an example of this profound change in the person, the Rav relates how even natural phenomena morph to become halakhic events. He writes:

If a Jew cognizes, for example, the Sabbath laws and precepts concerning the sanctity of the day in all their particulars, if he comprehends, via a profound study and understanding that penetrates to the very depth, the basic principles of Torah law that take on form and color within the tractate Shabbat, then he will perceive the sunset of the Sabbath eve not only as a natural phenomenon but as an eternal sanctity that is reflected in the setting of the sun. I remember how once, on the Day of Atonement, I went outside into the synagogue courtyard with my father (R. Moses Soloveitchik), just before the *Neilah* service. It had been a fresh, clear day, one the fine, almost delicate days of summer's end, filled with sunshine and light. Evening was fast approaching beyond the trees of the cemetery, into a sea of purple and gold. R. Moses, a halakhic man par excellence, turned to me and said: "This sunset differs from ordinary sunsets for with it forgiveness is bestowed upon us for our sins" (the end of the day atones). (HM, p. 38)

The Higher Longs for the Lower

Rabbi Soloveitchik concludes the chapter describing the most extreme dimension of Judaism's "this worldly" perspective. The Rav explains that the Torah, God's most exalted creation, is a book of the deepest wisdom about *this world*. Contrary to many other approaches within Judaism which see the Torah's laws and directives for life in this world as some type of hidden system by which higher realms are impacted for good or bad, the Rav explains that the Torah's perspectives is just the opposite. Not only is the Torah essentially a "this-world" system, but the higher realms of being recognize this and study the Torah in the way that a person would, dealing with the problems and issues that are unique to human life. The Rav writes:

When the righteous sit in the world to come, where there is neither eating nor drinking, with their crowns on their heads, and enjoy the radiance of the divine presence (cf. Berakhot 17a; Maimonides, *Laws of Repentance* 8:2), they occupy themselves with the study of the Torah, which treats of bodily life in our lowly world. "Now they were disputing in the heavenly academy this: If the bright spot (of the leper) preceded the white, he is defiled; if the reverse, he is clean. If (the order is) in doubt, the Holy One, blessed be He, ruled he is clean; while the entire heavenly academy ruled he is defiled."-Baba Metzia 86a...The Creator of worlds, revealed and unrevealed, the heavenly hosts, the souls of the righteous all grapple with halakhic problems that are bound up with the empirical world-the red cow, the heifer whose neck is to be broken, leprosy, and similar issues...The universal *homo religiosus* proclaims: The lower yearns for the higher. But halakhic man, with his unique mode of understanding, declares. The higher longs and pines for the lower. (HM, p. 38-39)

Chapter Eight

Halakhic man's profile has been presented to us. Now, Rabbi Soloveitchik returns to further clarify and deepen our understanding of the differences that distinguish halakhic man from cognitive man and homo religiosus, two ideal types with which halakhic man appears to share certain characteristics. Halakhic man focuses on the formulation and clarification of abstract systems, as well as the coordination of these abstractions with the real world. In this way he resembles cognitive man. But he also is God-obsessed and has at the center of his being and endeavors, a longing for closeness to God in all his transcendent perfection. The Rav states:

> On the one hand, as we explained above, his image resembles that of cognitive man, who occupies himself with intellectual constructions-experiencing all the while the joy of discovery and the thrill of creation-and then coordinating his ideal intelligible with the real world, as does the mathematician. And yet, on the other hand, halakhic man is not a secular, cognitive type, unconcerned with transcendence and total under the sway of temporal life. God's Torah has implanted in halakhic man's consciousness both the idea of everlasting life and the desire for eternity...His soul, too, thirsts for the living God, and these streams of yearning surge and flow to the sea of transcendence to "God who conceals Himself in His dazzling hiddenness" (the first line of a kabbalistic piyyut recited at the conclusion of the Sabbath meal). (HM, p. 39-40).

The Rav eloquently explains that, although halakhic man utilizes the methodology of the cognitive man in his abstract conception-building and application to the real world, his objectives and values are akin to that of the *homo religiosus*, but with one profound difference. Where the *homo religiosus* sees his objective as utilizing his mind and efforts to vault from this world to a higher and holier realm in which he draws close to God, halakhic man has as his objective the "bringing down" of holiness from these supernal realms of being and sanctifying temporal human life. The *homo religiosus* and the halakhic man are traveling the same path, but in different directions. Rabbi Soloveitchik writes:

> The only difference between homo religiosus and halakhic man is a change of courses-they travel in opposite directions. Homo religiosus starts out in this world and ends up in supernal realms; halakhic man starts out in supernal realms and ends up in this world. Homo religiosus, dissatisfied, disappointed, and unhappy, craves to rise up from the vale of tears, from concrete reality, and aspires to climb to the mountain of the Lord. He attempts to extricate himself from the narrow straits of empirical existence and emerge into the wide spaces of a pure and pristine transcendental existence. Halakhic man, on the contrary, longs to bring transcendence down into this valley of the shadow of death-i.e., into our world-and transform it into a land of the living. (HM, p. 40).

The Courage and Fortitude of Halakhic Man

It should be noted that there is courage found in the stance of halakhic man which is perhaps not present in the personality of the *homo religiosus*. Religion which focuses on the longing for the next world in its pristine perfection has an escapist dimension at its core. This world, with its flaws, disappointments, suffering and death, is "looked past" by the *homo religiosus* who keeps his "eye on the prize" of heaven and the world to come. This provides a solace and comfort to those who embrace it and do not focus their deepest attachment to this "flawed world" and endure this "vale of tears" for the good it will yield to the God-fearing after death.

In contrast to the above perspective, halakhic man holds fast to this world with all its pain and struggle to bring holiness into it and to sanctify it, as is God's will. Rabbi Soloveitchik writes:

> Halakhic man, however takes up his position in this world and does not move from it. He wishes to purify this world, not to escape from it. "Flight goeth before a fall. (Sotah 8:6)" Halakhic man is characterized by a powerful stiff-neckedness and stubbornness. He fights against life's evil and struggles relentlessly with the wicked kingdom and with all the hosts of iniquity in the cosmos. His goal is not flight to another world that is wholly good, but rather bringing down that eternal world into the midst of our world. (HM, p. 41)

The Rav warns that the "other-worldly" focus of religion often results in cruel and destructive outcomes for this world. Religion that views this world as simply a means to a greater end often makes decisions which torment those in this world to supposedly increase their rewards in the world to come. Much of mankind's history is the history of unspeakable cruelty carried out in the name of religion and the salvation of the soul for the sake of heaven.

> Homo religiosus, his glance fixed upon the higher realms, forgets all too frequently the lower realms and becomes ensnared in the sins of ethical inconsistency and hypocrisy. See what many religions have done to this world on account of their yearning to break through the bounds of concrete reality and escape to the sphere of eternity. They have been so intoxicated by their dreams of an exalted supernal existence that they have failed to hear the cries of "them that dwell in houses of clay" (Job 4:19), the sighs of orphans, the groans of the destitute. Had they not desired to unite with

infinity and to merge with transcendence, then they might have been able to do something to aid the widow and orphan, to save the oppressed from the hand of the oppressor. There is nothing so physically and spiritually destructive as diverting one's attention from this world. And, by contrast, how courageous is halakhic man who does not flee from this world, who does not seek to escape to some pure, supernal realm. (HM, p. 41)

Is Homo Religiosus Making A Mistake in His Method of Serving God?

Rabbi Soloveitchik does seem to me to find fault with *homo religiosus*'s methodology in its ability to serve the Creator and enhance his relationship with God. The Rav holds the *homo religiosus* accountable for underemphasizing the physicality of the human being and for underestimating the impact of his earthly nature in *homo religiosus's* enthusiasm to attach himself to God.

> Halakhic man knows that there is no royal road leading to the transcendent realm. Man's whole being is stamped with the indelible imprint of corporeality, concreteness, and sensation. And whither shall he go from their presence, and whither shall he flee from them? Yea, if he ascends to a heavenly existence, there will they be; yea, if he takes the wings of the abstract and the supernal, there would their hand lead him. Halakhic man does not believe that one who is held captive in the prison house of bodily existence can free himself from all vestiges of material existence, can snap the fetters of the body and the *yetzer* and ride in his majesty through the skies. (HM, p. 42)

The Exoteric Nature of Halakhic Man

Rabbi Soloveitchik describes the exoteric nature of the halakhic system. The term "exoteric" –the polar opposite of the better-known term "esoteric" is translated by Merriam-Webster as:

> 1. Suitable to be imparted to the public. 2. Belonging to the outer or less initiate circle.

The Jewish law is one that is applicable and available to everyone, regardless of wealth, status, or legal situation. No one is excluded from the practice or study of the law and all can reach the most exalted level of this process by becoming a great *Talmud chachum* (Torah scholar). The Rav is unequivocal in his rejection of any individual or group of individuals who have a special, mysterious connection to God through which others must mediate their approach and service of the Creator. It is through the Halakhah that every person serves God and through the observance and study of the Halakhah, that the person draws close to the Holy One. The Rav writes:

> Halakhic man's religious viewpoint is highly exoteric. His face is turned toward to the people. The Torah, whether in terms of study or practice, is the possession of the entire Jewish community. Everyone, from the judges and leaders of the people to the hewers of wood and drawers of water, is obliged to live in accordance with the Torah. "Ye are standing this day, all of you before the Lord your God: your leaders, your tribes, your elders, and your officers…from the hewer of thy wood unto the drawer of thy water" (Deut. 29;9-10) (HM, p. 42)

The role of the great *Talmud chachum* is to clarify for the individual how he or she can carry out the Halakhah and thereby approach God. This clarification and guidance providing by the *Talmud chachum* is instructive and a result of the knowledge he acquired through study. Any individual can travel the same path and become a *Talmud chachum* himself. In this the halakhic system resembles that of cognitive man and his study of science and mathematics. The great scientist has nothing but his knowledge of the system which provides him with his status and role as teacher and guide to others. It is nothing other than this knowledge of the system which allows him to instruct and lead others. Einstein did not have a special status as a human being per se. He simply understood and developed ideas for understanding the physical world in a more profound way. Once these were taught to others and they understood them as well as Einstein, they were the equivalent of Einstein with regard to their ability to teach and apply the ideas.

> ..."With three crowns was Israel crowned-with the crown of Torah, with the crown of the priesthood, and with the crown of royalty. Aaron acquired the crown of priesthood...David acquired the crown of royalty. The crown of the Torah, however is ready and available for all Israel, for it is written: 'Moses commanded us a law, an inheritance of the congregation of Jacob (Deut. 33:4). Whoever desires come and take it. (HM, p. 42)

Rabbi Soloveitchik contrasts the Halakhah's exoteric character with the esoteric element that many religious groups outside and inside of Judaism attach to the quest for closeness. They focus their efforts on contemplating and plotting a path to the world to come, viewing this world as coarse and evil. They set up intermediary individuals (different version of "holy men") who are supposedly endowed with unique spiritual qualities of their person which makes them indispensible to go through in order for others to connect to the Creator. The Rav rejects this as inauthentic with regard to Judaism and destructive to the followers of such individuals and the community which is led in this manner.

> A religiosity that center upon the heavenly kingdom and not upon the earthly kingdom-that can be made to reflect the heavenly kingdom-gives rise to ecclesiastical tyranny, religious aristocracies, and charismatic personalities. And there is nothing that the Halakhah loathes and despises as much as the idea of cultic mediation or the choosing of individuals, on the basis of supernatural consideration, to be intercessors for the community. (HM, p. 43)

The Rav revives here the issues of the validity of Hasidic rebbeim whose place in the Hasidic community is more than a teacher, incorporating a belief that the rebbe has some unique spiritual connection of an esoteric character and that, without him, the other member of the community are distant from God. Rabbi Soloveitchik writes:

> This exoteric approach is also the reason why many great halakhic scholars disapproved of the cult of the tzaddik in the Hasidic world. These great halakhic men had no sympathy for any practice which, in their opinion, contradicted such a fundamental halakhic principle as religious exoterism.

Halakhic Man and the Concept of Holiness

"Holiness" (*kedushah*) is central to Judaism and the general religious experience. But what precisely is meaning of the concept of "holiness" and how is it manifest in the Halakhah? Here too, Rabbi Soloveitchik explains, that the halakhic system rejects an "other-worldly" focus which is often the general approach to those who seek holiness in their lives. For the halakhic man holiness is not sought in higher realms but in the nitty-gritty existence of day-to-day life. The Rav writes:

> Holiness, according to the outlook of Halakhah, denotes the appearance of a mysterious transcendence in the midst of our concrete world, the "descent" of God, whom no thought can grasp, onto Mount Sinai, the bending down of a hidden and concealed world and lowering in onto the face of reality. Holiness does not wink at us from "beyond" like some mysterious star that sparkles in the distant heavens, but appears in our actual, very real lives...Holiness consists of a life ordered and fixed in accordance with Halakhah and finds its fulfillment in the observance of the laws regulating human biological existence, such as the laws concerning forbidden sexual relations, forbidden foods, and similar precepts. And it was not for naught that Maimonides included these prohibitions in his *Book of Holiness*. (HM, p. 46-47).

One of the most unexpected dimensions of the Rav's description of holiness is the human contribution. It is not God alone that renders an object or activity holy. As Rabbi Soloveitchik states: "Holiness is created by man, by flesh and blood." It is man acting in conjunction with God that is required for holy transformation. Without this human dimension holiness cannot reside on Earth. The Rav writes:

Through the power of our mouths, through verbal sanctification alone, we can create holy offering for the Temple treasury and holy offerings for the altar. The land of Israel became holy through conquest, Jerusalem, and the Temple courts-through bringing two loaves of thanksgiving (Jerusalem) or the remainder of the meal offerings (Temple court) and song, etc. (See Maimonides, Laws of the Sanctuary 6:11-16). It is man who sanctifies space and makes a sanctuary for his Creator. (HM, p. 47)

Moses and Solomon both struggled with the idea of how the infinite God could dwell among finite man in his finite space.

> Moses wondered: How is it possible to cause the absolutely transcendent, the Most High who dwells in concealment, the Almighty who abides in the deep darkness to reside in the midst of a small, narrow sanctuary, in the midst of the concrete world that is delimited by physical laws and the bounds of space and time?...This problem found its expression in the question of Solomon: "But will God in very truth dwell on earth?"...However God's answer is: "I am not of the same opinion as you. But twenty boards in the north and twenty in the south and eight in the west (the dimension of the sanctuary). And more than that, I will contract My divine presence in one square cubit." (HM: p. 47-48)

The Rav concludes this chapter with perhaps the most pivotal of experiences in which God miraculously "contracted" his infinite nature to accommodate the finite on Mount Sinai.

> It is Judaism that has given the world the secret of tzimtzum, of "contraction" contraction of the infinite within the realm of reality. When the Holy One, blessed by He, descended on

Mount Sinai, He set an eternally binding precedent that it is God who descends to man, not man who ascends to God. When He said to Moses, "And let them make Me a sanctuary, that I may dwell among them" (Exod. 25:8), He thereby revealed the awesome mystery that God contracts His divine presence in this world. (HM: p. 48).

Chapter Nine

In the ninth chapter of part one of "Halakhic Man" Rabbi Soloveitchik explores the underlying foundations of the Jewish mystical approach-particularly that of the Habad Hasidim and compares it to the perspective of halakhic man. This analysis is carried out through the analysis of the concept of *tzimtzum* ("contraction"). The Rav begins:

> This mystery of "tzimtzum", of "contraction," in the Halakhah does not touch upon questions of cosmology. Unlike the kabbalists and (*mutatis mutandis*-a Latin phrase meaning "generally speaking, but not exactly"-*RB*) Philo, Plotinus, the Neo-Platonoists, and the Renaissance philosophers, the Halakhah does not concern itself with metaphysical mysteries. Nor does it inquire into that which is too remote for it regarding the creation of the universe. The law of Halakhah is a practical-utilitarian one. Therefore one should not compare the concept of tzimtzum in the Halakhah with the concept as it appears in mystical doctrine. (HM, p. 49)

The concept of *"tzimtzum"* in halakhah allows for eternal to dwell within the finite. God, so to speak dwells in the limited confines of the Sanctuary and the Temple. God's presence in this world, allowing us to pray to Him and for His creations and miracles to manifest within time and space is the "utilitarian" dimension of *tzimtzum*. However, the concept of *tzimtzum* as understood by the kabbalists and Hasidim is a different one. The Rav now embarks on an explanation of the meaning of *tzimtzum* in the mystical teaching of the Habad Hasidim. Through this explanation the Rav attempts to establish clear lines of demarcation between the "this-world"-centered halakhic man and the "other-world" focus of the *homo religiosus*, exemplified here in the followers of Habad Hasidim.

> Therefore, one should not compare the concept of *tzimtzum* in the Halakhah with the concept as it appears in mystical doctrine. There (in mystical doctrine) this idea expresses a metaphysical system that penetrates into the hidden recesses of creation, that contemplates the foundation stones of the cosmos, being and nothingness, the beginning and the end; here (in Halakhah) the concept of *tzimtzum* does not pertain to the secrets of creation and the chariot but rather to law and judgment. Therefore, halakhic man's ontological outlook (perspective on existence- *RB*) differs radically from that of the mystic. (HM, p. 49)

What follows is a rare opportunity in which we can explore the Rav's insights regarding the concept of *tzimtzum* as understood by Habad Hasidim. Rabbi Soloveitchik carries out this exploration to clarify the divergence in the thinking of *homo religiosus* and halakhic man. Let us explore the Rav's analysis.

The Mystic's Perspective of Tzimtzum

Rabbi Soloveitchik reveals that the mystic views the world in a negative light. The foundation of the Jewish mystic's approach, as understood by the Kabbalah views the world's existence, as being due to a type of diminishment of God. The Rav writes:

> The mystic sees the existence of the world as a type of "affront," heaven forbid, to God's glory; the cosmos impinges upon the infinity of the Creator. The Kabbalah senses and empathizes with the anguish of the *Shekhinta be-galuta*, the Divine Presence in exile-the glory of God that emerged from the hiddenness of infinity, that became embodied in the creation of the cosmos, and that became contracted in it and by it. (HM, p. 49).

According to this understanding, for God to manifest his glory in the fullest sense, there can be nothing but God. For the universe to exist, God had to "contract" or diminish in some way his glory. This is a deep and subtle concept beyond the scope of this text, but perhaps we can explain it as God "shifting" so to speak from full actualization of His Being to a more potential state. As all hold God cannot change, this concept is certainly a difficult one. The Rav continues:

> The creation of the world constitutes a type of "waiver" on the part of God of His own glory, "for He is holy and separate from all the world and no thought can grasp Him." (*Likkutei Torah* –Vilna 1928: *Nitzavim*) The cosmos is a revelation of God's grace, "for His *Shekhinah*, His Divine Presence, clothes herself with worlds in order to give them life and impart existence to them. (Ibid)

The text of "Halakhic Man" emphasizes that for the mystic, the existence of the world, though the creation has an act of kindness by God to His creation, it has a "tragic" core, in that it diminished the glory of God. For God to become the "God of the world" he had to lessen in some way, beyond our understanding, His Existence. The Rav explains:

> The very grammatical for of "God of the world"-i.e., the genitive case-is a self-contradiction, a veritable coincidence of opposites. The world cannot exist when it is directly related to God. When God's splendid majesty shines forth and stands revealed, then everything reverts to chaos and the void. Therefore, mystical doctrine contemplates existence from a pessimistic perspective, and the ontological ideal is not its ultimate end. (HM, p. 50)

The "Tragic Trade-off" Necessary to Allow the Existence of the World

The world, according to the mystic approach explained here, exists as the result of a terrible "bargain" so to speak. The world existence comes at the expense of reducing God's glory. He must hide His glory away, so to speak, so that the world can exist in His presence. If I can be so bold as to give a few mundane allegories to help explain how I understand the concept:

1. To look directly at a solar eclipse would damage the eyes of the viewer so it is viewed indirectly to preserve the person's eye, but the beauty of beholding the solar eclipse in it full glory is diminished.

2. Imagine a song so beautiful that after being heard the person could never forget it or think of anything else. So to preserve the mind of the listener, the beauty of the song is diminished or hidden to a degree so that the listener can experience it in a lesser way, but the mind of the person remains intact.

3. In order for a brilliant mathematician to share his ideas with lesser minds, he simplifies it so that they can appreciate it at their level. If he explained it in its full detail and depth, the listeners would not be able to understand it at all.

These examples try to express the diminishment of something excellent so that it can be experienced in some manner by others. So too, God, according to the mystical understanding, diminishes the manifestation of His glory, so that the world can exist and experience God in a partial, hidden manner. Without this diminishment, there could be no sharing of existence with God and therefore no recognition of His glory.

The Mystic's Longing for the End of the Existence

The mystic, the Rav explains, reflecting this tragic situation of existence in which God, the Beloved is in a state of diminishment of His glory creates a sense of despair by which he, in a sense, desires the end of the existence and the beginning of a new stage where this diminishment will be rectified.

> Therefore, mystical doctrine contemplates existence from a pessimistic perspective, and the ontological ideal is not its ultimate end. It senses and empathizes with the anguish of the *Shekhinah*, of the Divine Presence, and longs to rise up together with her from the narrow straits of reality and to cleave to the most high God "who is exalted, lofty, and separate, all alone and not manifest in any other being." This, according to mystical teaching, is the glorious and exalted eschatological vision: "In that day shall the Lord be One, and His name One" (Zech. 14:9). And every day the mystic prays for the fulfillment of this aspiration as he recites before the performance of a commandment, "I am ready and prepared to carry out the commandment of my Creator for the sake of unifying the Holy One, blessed be He, with His *Shekhinah*, with His Divine Presence." (HM, p. 50-51)

So for the mystic there is a regret that co-exists with the joy and appreciation he has of God's creation of the world. It is an act of goodness and kindness, but one that comes, according to the mystic perspective, at the price of diminishing the ultimate Good-the glory of God.

The Ultimate Antinomy of God and Creation

An "antinomy" is defined as:

1. a contradiction between two apparently equally valid principles or between inferences correctly drawn from such principles
2. a fundamental and apparently irresolvable conflict or contradiction

This term applies well to the contradiction that seems to be at the root of the mystic's view of God's creation of the world. On the one hand, God had to "contract and hide" the full glory of His Being to allow for the existence of the world. On the other hand the world only was created and maintains its exist due to God's continued presence in the world. As the Rav explains:

> God, qua (as-*RB*) He who fills all worlds and He who encompasses all worlds, sustains the world; qua *Deus Absconditus,* the most hidden One, He who is above and beyond the mysterious, God nullifies the world and returns it to chaos and the void. The absolute contraction between existence and naught are only two faces that reveal themselves, as determined by the relationship between God and His creatures. (HM, p. 51)

Halakhic Man's Unambivalent Embrace of God's Creation

Rabbi Soloveitchik now contrasts halakhic man's full embrace of God's creation with that of *homo religiosus's* ambivalent attitude towards the world. The Rav writes:

> Halakhic man does not chafe against existence; rather he reads with the simplicity and innocence that is typical of him, the verse in Genesis, "And God saw everything that He had made, and, behold it was very good" (Gen. 1:31) and accepts

its verdict. He does not wish to free himself from the world, and he knows nothing about the idea of the Shekhina be-galuta, of the Divine Presence in exile, if taken to mean that the Divine Presence is held captive in the tresses of the cosmos and the chains of reality. He is completely suffused with an unqualified ontological optimism and is totally immersed in the cosmos. (HM, p. 51-52).

As opposed to the mystic's longing to unite his soul with God and of "unifying the Holy One, blessed be He, with His *Shekhinah*, with His Divine Presence", halakhic man longs to bring God's presence into the world to a greater degree. Rabbi Soloveitchik explains:

> ...the task of man is to bring down the Divine Presence to the lower world, to this vale of tears. The mystery of *tzimtzum* should not precipitate metaphysical anguish but rather gladness and joy. Man resides together with his Creator in this world, and it is only through cultivating that togetherness in the here and now that man can acquire a share in the world to come. The creation of the world does not inflict any "blemish" upon the idea of divinity, does not infringe upon infinity; on the contrary, it is the will of God that His *Shekhinah*, His Divine Presence, should contract and limit itself within the realm of empirical reality. (HM, p. 52)

In providing halakhic man's perspective on *tzimtzum* it appears that the Rav does not reject the idea as being invalid with regards to God's "contraction", only the perspective that this mysterious contraction of the infinite into the finite realm carries with it some tragic or negative outcome. Halakhic man views *tzimtzum* as an exceedingly positive dimension of existence through which G-d presence is experienced within the realm of human existence. He writes:

The mystery of *tzimtzum* should not precipitate metaphysical anguish but rather gladness and joy. Man resides together with his Creator in this world, and it is only through cultivating that togetherness in the here and now that man can acquire a share in the world to come. The creation of the world does not inflict any "blemish" upon the idea of divinity, does not infringe upon infinity; on the contrary, it is the will of God that His *Shekhinah*, His Divine Presence, should contract and limit itself within the realm of empirical reality. The great promised destiny "In that day shall the Lord be one, and His name one" (Zech. 14:9), instead of referring to the mystical dream of overcoming and negation of reality, refers to the era in which the Halakhah will find its fulfillment, its total realization in this world. (HM, p. 52)

The Creation of the World as God's Will

Rabbi Soloveitchik continues his comparison between the mystical perspective of Chabad Hasidim and halakhic man by citing an incident that occurred to the Rav's grandfather Rabbi Hayyim Soloveitchik in which the great rabbi commented on a fundamental concept regarding God's creation of the world. The Rav writes:

R. Simha Zelig, the disciple and friend of R. Hayyim, related to me the following incident: Once he and R. Hayyim visited someone's house in Vilna. While they were waiting for their host to appear, R. Hayyim glanced through some works of Habad Hasidism that were lying on the table. The books apparently discussed the question of God's motivation in creating the world and cited two opinions: (1) God created the world for the sake of His goodness; (2) He created the world for the sake of His grace. R. Hayyim turned to R. Simha Zelig and with utter seriousness told him: "Both views are incorrect, the world was created neither for the sake of His goodness, nor for the sake of His grace but for the sake of His will." (HM, p. 52)

The mystic sees an element of "sacrifice" by God in the creation of the world, as God "diminished", so to speak, the manifestation of His Glory to allow for its existence. This is the "goodness" or "grace" that motivated creation according to the mystic. Halakhic man views this as incorrect. The creation of the world and the mysterious *tzimtzum* it entailed was, according to halakhic man, God's absolute will and did not constitute a "Divine compromise" of any kind. Thus "the world was created for the sake of His will"-and not for the sake of His grace or His goodness. The Rav attributes this view the Rambam as discussed in his work "The Guide for the Perplexed."

Rabbi Soloveitchik reiterates this idea that the ideal place for the *Shekhinah*, the Divine Presence, is in this world and its departure from this world to higher, purer realms is the tragic situation. The Rav utilizes a commentary by Abba bar Kahana regarding the Garden of Eden to elucidate this point. He writes:

> The ideal of halakhic man is that the Divine Presence should rest here in this world. "And there I will meet with thee, and I will speak with thee from above the art-cover." (Exod. 25:22). This verse represents the ultimate telos of the Halakhah. "R. Aba bar Kahana said: It is not written in the text 'And they heard the voice of the Lord God walking (*mehalekh: pi'el* form) in the garden' but 'And they heard the voice of the Lord God skipping (*mithalekh: hitpa'el* form) in the garden' (Gen. 3:8). This (use of the reflexive) implies that He sprang ever upward (i.e., they heard God *departing* from the garden.) The abode of the Divine Presence was in the lower realms. As soon as Adam sinned, the Divine Presence betook itself to the first firmament; Cain sinned, it betook itself to the second firmament, the generation of Enosh to the third, the generation of the flood to the fourth; the

generation of the dispersion to the fifth; the Sodomites to the sixth; the Egyptians in the time of Abraham to the seventh. As a counterpart to these there arose seven righteous men who brought down the Divine Presence from above to below…Because of man's sins, the Divine Presence betook itself on high and the chosen of all human beings, Moses our teacher, brought it down below. The garden of God is this world not a supernal one." (HM, p. 54-55).

Halakhah and the Concretizing of Infinity

Rabbi Soloveitchik finds aspects of the mysterious concept of *tzimtzum* (contraction) within the halakhic system and its process of concretizing and quantifying the religious act. This process of meticulous quantification of halakhic law is viewed by many as being petty and pedantic, reducing the spiritual power of the religious experience. The Rav explains, that, on the contrary, this core principal of halakhah is part of the method by which Torah brings the holiness of the infinite in the finite dimension of life on earth. The Rav writes:

> The Halakhah, from the perspective of the process of contraction, also uses the method of quantification; it quantifies quality and religious subjectivity in the form of concrete, objective phenomena that are standardized and measurable. "The laws relating to standards, interpositions, and partitions are laws revealed to Moses on Mount Sinai" (Eruvin 4a; Sukkah 5b). The Halakhah fixes firmly established and clearly delimited laws, statutes, and measures for each and every commandment-what constitutes eating and what are its measurements, what constitutes drinking and what are its standards, what constitutes a fruit and what are its stages of development and distinguishing characteristics, the thirty-nine categories of work on the Sabbath and their measurements, the measurements of a tent

that defiles, partitions, units of monetary value, and many more. (HM, p. 55)

Halakhic Quantification of Reality and *Tzimtzum*

The Rav sees in this quantification of halakhah a manifestation of the process of *tzimtzum*. The Rav posits a convergence between the halakhic man's focus on the quantification of religious reality and the understanding of *tzimtzum* (contraction of the infinite in the finite) as understood by Habad Hasidism's greatest luminary, Rabbi Schneur Zalman. Rabbi Soloveitchik quotes Rabbi Zalman from his work *Likkutei Amarim, Igger Ha-Kodesh* (chapter 10, p. 115a):

> Now because the commandments were given to us by way of being clothed in the attribute of strength (*gevurah*-RB) and by the contraction of the light...therefore, most commandments have a delimited, 'contracted' measure. For instance, the length of the tzitzit (must be) twelve times the width of the thumb; the phylacteries, two fingers by two fingers and necessarily square; the lulav, four handbreaths, the sukkah, seven handbreaths; the shofar, one handbreath; the mikvah, forty se'ahs. Similarly, the 'sacrifices have a delimited, 'contracted' measure as regards age, as for instance, 'lambs of the first year'. (Exod. 29:38). (HM, p. 55-56)

The Rav comments on this:

> R. Shneur Zalman of Lyady, the founder of Habad Hasidism, that great luminary of Halakhah and mysticism, sensed that the fundamental method of the Halakhah is that act of quantification which is so integral a part of the mystery of *tzimtzum*. (HM, p. 56)

The Two Dimension of Creation That are Subject to Quantification

Rabbi Soloveitchik notes that the process of quantification is a fundamental tool utilized by the human mind in its quest understand reality. The quantification of perceptions and concepts plays a key role in the understanding of both the physical world of science and in the abstract world of halakhah. Both abstractions and concrete realities require this process of quantification to be rendered understandable and function. The Rav writes:

> God has introduced a parallelism; for just as the qualitative reality to which our senses are exposed lends itself to quantification by cognitive man, who turns qualities into quantities, precepts into equations, so, too, the supernal illumination "which may be perceived by means of the many mighty contractions which it undergoes as the different levels (of reality) emanates from one another," is placed within and under the dominion of the delimited, "contracted," quantitative act. The "movement" from quality to quantity, from experience to equations, which takes place in the real, empirical world, also finds its expression in the ideal realm of Halakhah. The statement of Galileo that "the great book which ever lies before our eyes-I mean the Universe-is written in mathematical language and the characters are triangles, circles, and other geometrical figures" applies as well to the Halakhah. (HM, p. 56-57).

The role of quantification in the area of Jewish law is often viewed by those outside the system as being an "interference" or "trivializing" of the religious act which are seen by these critics as needing to be more unrestricted in order to be meaningful and moving. Rabbi Soloveitchik rejects this perspective and defends the absolute need for the "quantification of the spirit" in order for religion to have its transformative impact on the individual and the community. The Rav states:

> A subjective religiosity cannot endure. And all those tendencies to transform the religious act into pure subjectivity negate all corporeality and all sensation in religious life and admit man into a pure and abstract world, where there is neither eating nor drinking, but religious individuals sitting with their crowns on their heads and enjoying their own inner experiences, their own tempestuous, heaven-storming spirits their own hidden longings and mysterious yearnings-will in the end prove null and void. The stychic power of religion that seizes hold of man, that subjects and dominates him, is in force only when the religion is a concrete religion, a religion of life of the senses, in which there is sight, smell, and touch, a religion which a man of flesh and blood can feel with all of his senses, sinews, and organs, with his entire being, a sensuous religion which conative man will encounter, in a very palpable way, wherever he may go. A subjective religiosity comprised of spiritual moods, of emotions and affections, of outlooks and desires, will never be blessed with success. (HM, p. 58)

As we have seen in the 21st century the unanticipated expanse of Orthodox Judaism and the equally dramatic contraction of the U.S. Conservative and Reform Jewish communities, these words from 1944 have proven to be accurate and prescient in their assessment.

Rabbi Soloveitchik's Criticism of Maimonides View of *Piyyutim*

At this point in the essay Rabbi Soloveitchik criticizes Maimonides negative view of *piyyutim*. These are Jewish liturgical poems sung or chanted during the Temple or synagogue service. Maimonides opposed the recital of piyyutim due to their anthropomorphic portrayal of God. He writes in his "Guide for the Perplexed":

> Thus what we do (in prayer) is not like what is done by the truly ignorant who spoke at great length and spent great efforts on prayers that they composed and on sermons that they compiled... In these prayers and sermons they predicate of God qualitative attributions that if predicated of a human individual, would designate a deficiency in him...This kind of license is frequently taken by poets and preachers or such as they think what they speak is poetry, so that the utterances of some...contain rubbish and perverse imaginings. (HM, p.58 quoting from Guide, I, 59).

The Rav understands that the Halakhah, being focused on the human being's life in the physical world does not follow the Rambam's approach of not utilizing anthropomorphism in prayers to God. The concretization of the spiritual life in quantifiable, tangible halakhic structures, the Rav seems to include, to some extent, the concretizing of our conception and imaginings of the Creator, although they may not be accurate from a logical and philosophical perspective. Rabbi Soloveitchik writes:

> The Halakhah does not deem it necessary to reckon with speculative concepts and very fine, subtle abstractions on the one hand and vague feelings, obscure experiences, inchoate affections, and elusive subjectivity on the other. It determines law and judgment in Israel. (HM, p. 59)

Halakhah and the Structuring of Human Inner Experience

Rabbi Soloveitchik extends the concretizing of Halakhah from the realm of action to that of human thought. The Halakah provides boundaries and orderliness to the powerful, surging energy of the religious experience.

But instead of seeing this as a limiting or stilting of the spirit, the Rav explains that it transforms dangerous, undefined and uncontrolled religious longing into one that enlightens and beautifies the individual and the community, while enduring the vicissitudes of life. The Rav writes:

> The Halakhah wishes to objectify religiosity not only through introducing the external act and the psychophysical deed into the world of religion but also through the structuring and ordering of the inner correlative in the realm of man's spirit. The Halakhah sets down statutes and erects markers that serve as a dam against the surging, subjective current coursing through the universal homo religiosus, which, from time to time, in its raging turbulence sweeps away his entire being to obscure and inchoate realms. (HM, p. 59)

Rabbi Soloveitchik explains this dichotomy in elucidating the state of mind that is required of a person as they are about to perform a positive commandment (*mitzvah asay*). The Rav rejects the mystical approach of having in mind to perform the commandment for the sake of some impact it will have in the heavenly realm through which God will be reunited with his *Shekinah* (Divine Presence) or something else beyond this earthly realm. The Rav holds strongly with the simple intention by the individual performing a commandment that he or she is performing a commandment of God. It is an earthly act in obedience and recognition of the Creator. Nothing else is required. The Rav writes:

> The intention accompanying the performance of a commandment appears in the Halakhah illumined by the light of objectivity and lawfulness...Certainly, therefore, we should wholly abolish reciting mystical intentions. And it suffices to perform the commandment for the sake of the

> commandment...And any commandment which is not preceded by a blessing, my practice is to recite beforehand 'I am performing this action in order to fulfill the commandment of my Creator.' And the intention (required for prayer) is simply understanding the meaning of the words. All great halakhic scholars have acted in accordance with this decision. (HM, p. 60)

Rabbi Soloveitchik recounts an occurrence in which his father, Rav Moshe Soloveitchik made this position clear in his interaction with a shofar-blower on Rosh Hashanah who was a follower of Habad Hasidim and their mystical approach to the performance of commandments. The Rav writes:

> Once my father was standing on the synagogue on the synagogue platform on Rosh Hashanah, ready and prepared to guide the order of the sounding of the *shofar*. The *shofar*-sounder, a God-fearing Habad Hasid who was very knowledgeable in the mystical doctrine of the "Alter Rebbe," R. Shneur Zalman of Lyady, began to weep. My father turned to him and said: "Do you weep when you take the *lulav*? When then do you weep when you sound the *shofar*? The mystic understands the symbolic significance of the sounding of the *shofar*-the concept of a plain note-whereby man attempts to pierce through lawful existence and reach the throne of glory of the *Atik Yomim*, the Ancient One, the *Deus Absconditus*. The sounding of the *shofar*, according to the outlook of R. Shneur Zalman, expresses the powerful aspiration of *homo religiosus* to extricate himself from the straits of contraction-the divine realm of strength-and enter into the wide spaces of expansion-the divine realm of grace-and from thence to rise about the seven lower divine realms, "the cornerstones of the (cosmic structure)" into the hidden world in which the light of the Ein-Sof, the completely hidden infinite God, gleams and shines, as it were. Man's weeping on Rosh Hashanah, according to this doctrine, is the weeping of the soul that longs for its origin, for the rock from whence

it was hewn, that yearns to cleave to its beloved not in hiding, but openly. (HM, p.62)

The Rav contrasts the mystic's other-worldly focus when carrying out a mitzvah with that of halakhic man. He explains:

> Not so is the manner of halakhic man! He does not wish to snap the fetter of the objective form and demolish the iron bars of the firm and fixed lawfulness of this world. The *Shekhinah*, the Divine Presence, does not anguish over the mystery of tzimtzum, over her descent into the empirical realm; accordingly, halakhic man does not wish to free either her or himself from this realm. (HM, p.63)

Rabbi Soloveitchik's describes halakhic man's perspective on *shofar*-blowing as contrasting with that of *homo religiosus*. Where homo religiosus understands the *shofar*-blowing as a vehicle to remove one's spirit from this world and cleave to God in the higher realms, halakhic man sees it as a commandment to enhance and sanctify the earthly life by bringing the awareness and presence of God to a place of prominence and clarity in this earthly world.

Chapter Ten

The Rav continues his elucidation of halakhic man in this chapter with a focus on the normative dimension of his personality. Up to this point Rabbi Soloveitchik has clarified the ontological uniqueness of halakhic man. I will define and discuss the terms "ontological" and "normative" at this point as they are essential to understanding this chapter and are used throughout the essay. Ontology is defined as:

1: the branch of metaphysics which is concerned with the nature and the relations of being. 2: a particular theory about the nature of being or the kinds of things that have existence.

Ontology and the adjective "ontological" is the study of the underlying nature of reality or of existence. So for the *homo religiosus*, the ontological perspective is on the higher, purer realms of existence and a focus on God in His full glory. For the halakhic man, the ontological focus is on the nature of earthly existence and infusing this earthly reality with holiness (kedusha) through the living of a life aligned with God's will and an in consonance with His revealed truth in the Torah.

The term "normative" in contrast to the term "ontological" is defined as 1: of, relating to, or determining <u>norms</u> or standards (*normative* tests). 2: conforming to or based on norms (*normative* behavior, *normative* judgments).

A "norm" is a defined as follows: an authoritative standard : a principle of right action binding upon the members of a group and serving to guide, control, or regulate proper and acceptable behavior (No society lacks *norms* governing conduct —Robert K. Merton)

With regard to halakhic man, the normative dimension of his personality is how the norms of halakhah-its laws governing action and, to some degree, thought, constitute his underlying nature and in a sense become to underlying structure of the mind and personality of halakhic man. The halakhic man is more than a man (or woman) that adheres to the commandments and customs of the halakhic system of laws. The halakhic man is so invested in the Halakhah that it becomes the lens and the categories through which he cognizes and interacts with the world. The system of Halakhah and the man merge to become halakhic man. Rabbi Soloveitchik explains:

> Halakhic man cognizes the world in order to subordinate it to religious performances. For instance, he cognizes space by means of religious, a priori, lawful categories in order to realize in it the halakhic norm of Sabbath, commandment of sukkah, and the idea of purity...Thus his normative doctrine has priority, from a teleological perspective, over his ontological approach. Cognition is for the purpose of doing. "Great is study, for study leads to action" (Kiddushin 40b). (HM, p. 63)

> ...we have (in halakhic man-*RB*) a blending of the obligation with self-consciousness, a merging of the norm with the individual, and a union of an outside command with the inner will and conscience of man. (HM, p. 65)

The Rav continues to clarify this normative focus of halakhic man by explaining that, althrough his focus is on the normative system of halakhah, the halakhic man values the abstract absolute halakhic formulation over the application of the halakhah to the actual carrying out of halakhic activities. The Rav writes:

> Halakhic man is not particularly concerned about the possibility of actualizing the norm in the concrete world. He wishes to mint an ideal, normative coin. Even those laws that are not practiced in the present time are subjected to his normative viewpoint, this despite the fact that he is unable nowadays to fulfill these particular commandments. The maxim of the sages "Great is study, for study leads to action" has a twofold meaning:
>
> 1. action may mean determining the Halakhah or ideal norm;
> 2. action may refer to implementing the ideal norm in the real world.
>
> Halakhic man prioritizes action in its first meaning...

After explaining this valuing of the abstract Halakhah over the actual halakhah, Rabbi Soloveitchik returns to his description of the halakhic man's building his personality and mind upon the categories of Halakhah. For this reason halakhic man, unlike the *homo religiosus* or the cognitive man, is not tormented or pained by adherence to the halakhic norms. It is a natural activity that is aligned with his basic nature. The Rav explains:

> Unlike the Christian saints whose lives consisted of a long series of battles with the dazzling allure of life, with carnal, this-worldly pleasures, the great Jewish scholars know nothing about man's conflict with the evil urge. The church fathers devoted themselves to religious life in a state of

compulsion and duress, the Jewish sages in a state of joy and freedom...Thus King David, who said..."I will delight myself in Thy commandments, which I have loved...This is my comfort in my affliction, that Thy word hath quickened me." (Psalm 119:47, 50)

Rabbi Soloveitchik now touches the joyful, creative dimension of halakhic man's situation. Although the Halakhah is a revelation given to humanity from God, there is an essentially creative dimension to Torah study and the precise formulation of the Halakhah. The halakhic scholar does not simply learn a fixed body of laws, but instead participates creatively in the full formulation and completion of the halakhah and in its application to a varied and changing world. The Rav writes:

> When halakhic man comes to the real world, he has already created his ideal, a priori image, which shines with the radiance of the norm. The real world does not impose upon him anything new, nor does it compel him to perform any new action of which he had not been aware beforehand in his ideal world. And this ideal world is his very own, his own possession; he is free to create in it, to arrive at new insights, to improve and perfect. Spiritual freedom and intellectual independence reign there in unlimited fashion. Consequently, it seems to him as though this ideal world is his own creation. (HM, p. 65-66)

Chapter Eleven

Rabbi Soloveitchik continues to explore the overall personality differences between halakhic man and *homo religiosus*. The Rav explains that the *homo religiosus* focus his attention on the subjective experience of reality and the blurring of the boundaries of the higher realms with the lower realms of existence, differing from both halakhic man and cognitive man. The Rav writes about *homo religiosus*:

> The tendency toward subjectivity, toward the blurring of forms and boundaries, towards the confusion of domains-the lower with the higher, the corporeal with the spiritual, the revealed with the concealed... (HM, p. 66)

Halakhic man, on the other hand, tends towards the objective and clearly defined lawful aspects of the halakhic reality he experiences, establishing firm boundaries and a clear understanding. In this focus on the categorical, halakhic man resembles the objective-seeking nature of cognitive man. Halakhic man has a:

> Thrust toward objectivity and lawfulness, toward a firmly established creation, well formed, possessing boundaries, statutes, and judgments... (HM, p. 66)

There is a certain emotional distance and dispassionate aspect to the cognitive man and the halakhic man when they approach the worlds they want to understand. They both do not want to be:

> disqualified as an interested party ... not concerned in advance with the results of his cognition and study; he is but "a watchman and scout, a scribe, recorder and enumerator"

(terms from the Musaf prayer of Rosh Hashanah). (HM, p. 66)

The Rav contrasts this detached perspective of halakhic man with the passionate and intense emotional investment of the *homo religiosus* in his serving of God. He writes:

> This is not the case with *homo religiosus*! When he stands before the cosmos, he is entirely aflame with the holy fire of wonder, he is all ashudder, confronted with the incomprehensible and unknown. His soul rages and storms like a tempestuous sea. He is frightened-nay terrified-by the mystery. He hides is face, for he is afraid to look upon it. He flees from it, but at the same time, against his will, he draws near to it; enchanted, he finds himself irresistibly pulled toward it, pines for it, and longs to merge with it. (HM, p. 67)

The Tragic Aspect of the *Homo Religiosus*

Rabbi Soloveitchik presents the *homo religiosus* as vacillating between a fascination and love that draws him irresistibly towards God. When in the throes of this desire, he longs to break through all barriers to approach and merge his existence with that of the Creator. But the drawing close to God stimulates a feeling of dread and anxiety. In approaching this merging with God, *homo religiosus* senses the annihilation of his sense of personal identity. This causes him to retreat in terror and fear. The Rav writes:

> *Homo religiosus* is suspended between two giant magnets, between love and fear, between desire and dread, between longing and anxiety. His is caught between two opposing forces-the right hand of existence embraces him, the left thrusts him aside. Indeed, there is a great deal of truth in the view of Otto (Rudolph Otto – author of the text "The Idea of the Holy"-*RB*) that fascination and repulsion constitutes the

two fundamental experiences of *homo religiosus*. (HM, p. 67)

This dichotomy of fear and love results in the *homo religiosus* experiencing an existence of continual shifts between delight and anguish, between torment and wonder. There is a strong dose of self-infliction of pain in this life, but a pain that is desired as it is associated with drawing close to God. The Rav continues:

> He undergoes terrible pains in the search for the enigma that will only darken reality even more in the quest for a cognition that will only deepen the wonder, but at the same time he delights in those pains. At times homo religiosus is a masochist picking away at his own wounds and reveling in his own pain. These pains contain within themselves the sweetness of eternity, a taste of the world to come. The enjoyment of pain and delight in suffering can bring him to religious ecstasy. (Ibid.)

As a result of *homo religiosus's* intensely conflicting forward movement towards and retreat from God, he experiences a split sense of self with two divergent characteristics. As one who approaches merger with God, the *homo religiosus* has a sense of his greatness and exalted place in existence. But as he approaches God with some degree of proximity, he immediately realizes his own nothingness, inadequacy and sin and experiences a sense of himself as the lowest of all creatures in God' creation. The Rav explains:

> One the one hand, he senses his own lowliness and insignificance, his own frailty and weakness; he knows that even "a gnat preceded him, a snail preceded him." He sees himself as the one biological creature who has misused his

own talents for destructive ends, who has failed in the task assigned to him. On the other hand, he is aware of his own greatness and loftiness, his own spirit breaks through all barriers and ascends to the very heights, bores through all obstacles and descends to the very depth. (HM, 67-68)

The Rav portrays this conflict of man's sensing his nothingness on the one hand, and his exaltedness on the other by using two verses from Psalms, each describing man's essence in starkly contrasting terms. He writes:

> One verse declares, "When I behold Thy heavens, the work of Thy fingers, the moon and the stars which Thou hast established; what is man, that Thou are mindful of him, and the son of man, that thou thinkest of him?" (Ps. 8: 4-5), while the other verse declares, "Yet Thou hast made him but a little lower than the angels, and hast crowned him with glory and honor. Thou hast made him to have dominion over the works of Thy hands; Thou hast put all things under his feet. (Ps. 8:6-7). (HM, p. 68)

But halakhic man, the Rav explains "has found a third verse-the Halakhah". Rabbi Soloveitchik is utilizing, poetically, the method used in the learning of Torah where there are two seemingly contradictory Biblical passages about something and a third verse is brought to resolve the contradiction. Halakhic man also brings " a third verse" to resolve the contraction of these two verses from the Psalms which seems to present man as both exalted and as nothing. The "third verse" is the Halakhah. Through the study and practice of the halakhah man's value in confirmed. This exalted involvement by which God's will is known and actualized in His world on Earth is the involvement that transforms the nothingness of man into something of great meaning and value. The Rav writes:

Indeed, I am the one creature in this world who reflects the image of Divine Presence. Do I not study the Torah, the cherished plaything (see Ps. 119:77) of the Holy One, blessed be He? The angels themselves long to learn Torah from me! Am I not at this very moment reaching out to my lover and beloved? Halakhic man immediately discovers his redemption and the endorsement of his existence in this awareness and begins: "Thou hast chosen man at the very inception and Thou hast recognized him as worthy of standing before Thee." In a single moment his stature is so enhanced that he feels he can touch the very heavens! In the blinking of an eye the lowliest of creatures turns into the noblest of creatures, whom the Holy One, blessed be He, elected at the very inception and recognized as worthy of standing before Him. (HM. p. 70).

Halakhic man's perspective is that God's giving of His law to mankind is a clear confirmation of earthly man's position as a being of worth. Without man's participation in the Halakhah it would be true that his worth would be judged on its own merit and as such, he would be nothing. But with his acceptance, study and performance of the Torah, he becomes a being of renown and holiness-one that is close to God and a partner with the Source of all Being and all Good. The Rav writes:

The man who does not live according to the Halakhah and who does not participate in the realization of the ideal world is of no worth. "Before I was formed I was of no worth, and now that I have been formed it is as if I have not been formed. Dust I am in my life, and all the more in death" (conclusion of the Ne'ilah prayer). However, the man who knows his duty, his task as a partner in the creation of the worlds through constructing a halakhic world and actualizing it in reality has been elected by God at the very inception and has been recognized as worthy of standing before Him. (HM, p.71)

The Rav concludes this chapter with an insight into one of the most enigmatic verses in the Talmud where it is written.

> It were better for man not to be created than to have been created, but now that he has been created, let him examine his past deeds. (Talmud, Eruvin, 13B) (HM, p. 71-72)

Rabbi Soloveitchik understands this statement to mean that without Torah and its process of repentance and refinement, a man's life is of no value ("it were better for man not to be created than to be created"). But *with* the Torah, a person's life becomes worthy of existence and he is transformed into a holy being who related to God and carries out His will by transforming himself through repentance and the world he inhabits through applying the Halakhah to bring holiness into the world. The end of the phrase, "let him examine his past deeds", addresses these noble and blessed activities.

Chapter Twelve

In this chapter Rabbi Soloveitchik delves into the role of the Halakhah as a guardian of halakhic man against the feelings of despair and fear that plague the minds of *homo religiosus* and those who do not incorporate the halakhic system into their personality and mind. Although the Rav agrees that all human beings wrestle with existential issues such as the fear of death and nothingness, the halakhic man has a perspective that quells these torments in a constructive and meaningful way. He writes:

> Halakhic man knows no fear or dread in the full sense of the term. When he approaches the world, he is armed with his weapons-i.e., his laws-and the consciousness of lawfulness and order that is implanted within him serves to ward off the fear that springs upon him...Halakhic man does not give any thought to the "other side," that *tertium quid* (third element-*RB*) of being and nothingness. He is unfamiliar with the dark back streets of defilement, nor does he ever go astray in the blind alleys and narrow pathways of the world's emptiness and chaos. All stands before him, beautiful, finished, and adorned. Halakhic man is a man of the law and the principle, a man of the statute and judgment, and, therefore, he always possesses in his being, even if at times it should be afflicted with a deep melancholy, a fixed, firm, Archimedean point that is outside and above the turbulence of his soul, beyond the maelstrom of the affective life, a true source of peace and tranquility. (HM, p. 72-73).

Even the fear of death is blunted and transformed by the study of Halakhah. The Rav relates how when his grandfather, the great Talmudic scholar, Rabbi Hayyim Soloveitchik was overcome by a fear of death, he would throw himself wholeheartedly into the study of the Jewish laws related to death and would, through this study, transition from feelings of despair and anguish to joy and mastery. He writes:

> Halakhic man vanquishes even the fear of death, which, as was explained above, is rooted in his world perspective, by means of the law and the Halakhah, and he transforms the phenomenon which so terrified him, into an object of man's observation and cognition. For when death becomes the object of man's cognition, the fright, accompanying death dissipates…My father related to me that when the fear of death would seize hold of R. Hayyim, he would throw himself, with his entire heart and mind, into the study of the laws of tents and corpse defilement. And these laws, which revolve about such difficult and complex problems as defilement of a grave, defilement of a tent, blocked-up defilement, interposition before defilement, a vessel with a tight fitting cover upon it in a tent in which a corpse lies, etc,. etc., would calm the turbulence of his soul and would imbue it with a spirit of joy and gladness. (HM, p. 73).

How does this internal transformation take place? In studying the halakhic dimension of death, the halakhic man gains a sense of mastery over death and transforms it into something that he has mastery over through his logical dissection of its role in the system of Jewish laws. I believe the Rav uses death here as the ultimate test and example of how halakhah places all aspects of halakhic man's experience under the dominion of his analytic mind, robbing life's most daunting experiences of their ability to overwhelm and terrorize the human being. As the Rav states:

> Knowledge, by definition, is the subjugation of the object and the domination of the subject." (HM, p. 73)

Rav Hayyim and Rabbi Salanter – A Meeting of Halakhic Man and *Homo Religiosus*

Rabbi Soloveitchik exemplifies and humanizes the contrast between halakhic man and *homo religiosus* through a meeting that occurred between Rav Hayyim Soloveitchik, halakhic man *par excellence*, and R. Isaac Blaser, a representative of Rabbi Salanter's Mussar program who wanted to introduce this method into Yeshiva Volozhin, which Rav Hayyim led with Rabbi Naftali Zevi Yehudah Berlin. The Rav describes the essential character of the *Mussar* program and how it contrasted with the optimistic perspective of halakhic man:

> This movement at the beginning of its growth, symbolized the world perspective of the universal homo religiosus, a perspective directed toward the transcendent, toward that existence lying beyond the realm of concrete reality. The emotion of fear, the sense of lowliness, the melancholy so typical of homo religiosus, self-negation, constant self-appraisal, the consciousness of sin, self-lacerating torments, etc., etc., constituted the primary features of the movement's spiritual profile in its early years…The halakhic man of Brisk and Volozhin sensed that this whole mood posed a profound contradiction to the Halakhah and would undermine its very foundations. Halakhic man fears nothing. For he swims in the sea of Talmud, that life-giving sea to all the living. If a person has sinned, then the Halakhah of repentance will come to his aid. One must not waste time on spiritual self-appraisal, on probing introspections, and on the picking away at the "sense of sin"…Such a psychic analysis brings man neither to fear nor to love of God nor, most fundamental of all, to the knowledge and cognition of the Torah. The Torah cannot be acquired in a state of melancholia and depression. (HM, 74)

Halakhic Man's State of Equilibrium

The happiness of halakhic man is a bounded happiness. Just as the Halakhah guards him from the excesses of melancholy and depression, it too keeps him clear of excessive joy. The state of halakhic man is that of a stable, pleasant emotional equilibrium. The filter of halakhah through which he experiences the world, operates within this function emotional zone. The Rav writes:

> But is halakhic man stays clear of melancholy and dread, he also recoils from any exaggerated spirit of joy, any sense of celebration lacking a healthy logical foundation, and any spiritual drunkenness... This stance prevents man from being attracted to any of the extremes of the emotional life and places a bar against his spirit, which tends at times to shatter all bounds of restraint and control...his affective life is characterized by a fine equilibrium, a stoic tranquility. It exemplifies the Aristotelian golden mean and the ideal of the well-balanced personality set forth by Maimonides; it is guided by the knowledge of inevitability and the means of triumphing over it provided by the rule of Halakhah.

The system of halakhah to which halakhic man gives his full focus and adherence, regulates feelings as well as actions and requires the maintaining of a presence of mind that allows the adherent to fully comply with its requirements. The Halakhah, in a sense "becomes the man", thus "halakhic man". The Rav provides a moving story about the Vilna Gaon exemplifying how the halakhic man experiences even the most powerful of emotional states through the halakhic lens. He writes:

> It is related concerning the Gaon of Vilna how greatly he would rejoice on Simhat Torah during the *hakafot* (circular

processions with the Torah scroll-RB). He would dance, clap, sing and celebrate the occasion in a state of great rapture and enthusiasm. However, immediately afterward, upon the conclusion of the *hakafot*, he would revert back to his normal tranquil state. When the Gaon's brother died and the Gaon learned of it on the Sabbath (when mourning is forbidden), he did not display any emotion or signs of grief. After the Sabbath, when he concluded the *havdalah* he burst into tears.(HM, p. 77)

Chapter Thirteen

The "Self" of Halakhic Man and *Homo Religiosus*

Rabbi Soloveitchik turns in this chapter to the concept of self and that, while *homo religiosus* longs to lose his sense of self in the Great Self of God, halakhic man guards the integrity of his unique self. Halakhic man sees no contradiction between this strong sense of individuality and his total dedication to the fulfilling of God's will through the Halakhah. The Rav writes:

> The will of *homo religiosus* gradually wanes to nothingness, and his selfhood is inexorably extinguished inasmuch as he desires to immerse himself in the totality of existence and to unite with infinity. Halakhic man, however, protects his own selfhood, his particularity, his soul's private domain. The "I", the self, is also part of that concrete reality which Halakhah purified and hallowed. In general, wherever the moral law reigns supreme, the sense of individuality becomes deeper and stronger. (HM, p. 78).

The Rav relates this difference in the sense of self to the difference in the role of the moral law for Halakhic man and *homo religious*. While *homo religiosus* assesses the quest for a moral life and the perfection of the personality as secondary to the merging of the self with God, the halakhic man sees this as the primary human objective. The Rav explains:

> Even when he (*homo religiosus*) makes a supreme effort to scale the transcendental heights, the effort is not motivated by a desire to perfect his individuality. The opposite is true. What *homo religiosus* wants in *unio mystica*, (union with God-*RB*) attachment to infinity and complete immersion and dissolution in the supernal realm. In contrast to *homo*

religiosus, halakhic man forges for himself a concrete, this worldly personality. The maxim of Kant-that the moral law gives man the strength to stand before the overpowering cosmic drama without losing his own selfhood (Ibid.)

The Intellect of Halakhic Man and *Homo Religiosus*

Similarly, the *homo religiosus* and halakhic man differ in their perspectives regarding the human intellect. Whereas *homo religiosus* views the intellect ambiguously due to its being an impediment standing between him and his desired merger, with God, the halakhic man views it as his most precious possession as it is the means towards his understanding of God's law. The Rav writes:

> He (halakhic man) approaches the world of Halakhah with his mind and intellect, just as cognitive man approaches the natural realm. And since he relies upon his intellect, he places his trust in it and does not suppress any of his psychic faculties in order to merge into some supernal existence. His own personal understanding can resolve the most difficult and complex problems. (HM, p. 79).

The Humility of *Homo Religiosus* and Halakhic Man

The Rav portrays the halakhic man as a confident, bold and creative personality who revels in the world he inhabits as he assesses its halakhic challenges and obligations and impacts his environment to bring the halakhic ideal to fruition. There is no pervading sense of sin or self-loathing in him, as opposed to the *homo religiosus* who views this world with a much more ambivalent attitude. Rabbi Soloveitchik explains:

> Halakhic man is a spontaneous, creative type. He is not particularly submissive and retiring, and is not meek when it

is a matter of maintaining his own views. Neither modesty nor humility characterizes the image of halakhic man. On the contrary, his most characteristic feature is strength of mind. (Ibid.)

The Rav speaks here of halakhic man's lack of modesty/humility specifically in the role as halakhic thinker and actor. The halakhic man senses his self-importance is carrying out this role and will not be deterred in this holy quest. Shockingly, even God cannot deter man from his God-given right as halakhic authority. The Rav quotes the Talmud which portrays this attitude in the starkest of terms. He writes:

> This autonomy of the intellect at times reaches heights unimaginable in any other religion. The Talmud in Bava Metzia (86a) relates that there was a dispute between the Holy One, blessed be He, and the heavenly academy regarding a case where there is a doubt as to whether the bright spot (of a leper) proceeded the white hair or the white hair preceded the bright spot. The Holy One, blessed be He, ruled: He is clean, while the heavenly academy ruled He is unclean. And who was the arbiter (decider)? Rabbah bar Nahman. Flesh and blood, mortal man decides between the Holy One, blessed be He, and the heavenly academy. When there was a dispute between R. Eliezer and the sages regarding the purity of the oven of Aknai, a heavenly voice declared: "Why do you disagree with R. Eliezer, seeing that in all matters the Halakhah is in accordance with his ruling?" R. Joshua arose and said: " 'It is not in heaven' (Deut. 30:12)...For the Torah has already been given from Mount Sinai and we pay no attention to a heavenly voice." And the Holy One, blessed be He, smiled in that hour and said: 'My children have defeated Me, My children have defeated Me." (Babba Metzia, 59b) (HM, p. 79-80)

Halakhah has been given by God to man and now it is in the domain and control of halakhic man. This is God's will and the source of halakhic man's sense of self-worth and his bold, energetic stance towards living. The Rav writes:

> Halakhic man is a mighty ruler in the kingdom of spirit and intellect. Nothing can lead him astray; everything is subject to him, everything is under his sway and heeds his command. Even the Holy One, blessed be He, has, as it were, handed over His imprimatur, His official seal in Torah matters, to man; it is as if the Creator of the world Himself abides by man's decision and instruction. (HM, p. 80)

The Creative Role of Halakhic Man

Halakhic man's intellectual quest is a passive one. His role is not simply to receive, understand and carry out the law of God. Halakhic man is called upon to play an essentially creative role. Creative interpretation of the law in its application to the myriad of situations which arise in the human experience is required for the Halakhah to function as a living system. This creative intellectual involvement (*hiddush*), the Rav explains, is not a minor element of the halakhic man's activity. It is at the very core of his quest.

> Halakhic man received the Torah from Sinai not as a simple recipient but as a creator of worlds, as a partner with the Almighty in the act of creation. The power of creative interpretation (hiddush) is the very foundation of the received tradition. When Moses ascended on high, he found the Holy One, blessed be He, sitting there tying crowns to the letters in order that future generations should, by virtue of their powers of creative interpretation, discover heaps upon heaps of law contained in every tittle. (see Menahot 29b)..."Only man is capable of creative interpretation (hiddush), something which is beyond the power of angels, for since the Holy One, blessed be He, created them in a state of perfection, they need not and, therefore, cannot develop and progress. But this is

not the case with man, for he professes and his intellect gains ever-increasing strength...The essence of the Torah is intellectual creativity. (HM, p. 82)

Rabbi Soloveitchik concludes this chapter with a surprising reference. Rav Hayyim Volozhin's famous text *Nefesh ha-hayyim*, discusses, among other subjects, how the higher realms of existence are impacted by what takes place here on earth. Although this seems to me to be a focus that is very different than the concern of halakhic man (who focuses on the value of earthly life in its own right), the Rav cites it here to bring out the importance and, in some ways, superiority of earthly life over that of higher levels of existence. Rabbi Soloveitchik concludes:

> R. Hayyim Volozhin devoted the first chapter of his work *Nefesh ha-hayyim* to an explanation of the verse "And God created man is His own image, in the image of God created He him" (Gen. 1:27). The gist of his world perspective, to which he gives expression in his explanation, is that it is man who gives life to and constructs the worlds that are above him. (Ibid.)

The Rav explains in a footnote to the above statement that this is the meaning of the verse "And God created man in His image, in the image of God created He him" (Gen. 1:27).

> Just as God orders and guides the actions of these worlds at every moment in accordance with His will, so He, in accordance with His will, gave man dominion so that he might control myriads of forces and worlds in accordance with the particulars of the order of his actions in all his affairs at literally each and every moment...(Ibid.)

Here we see the "secret" of halakhic man's sense of his great worth. It is as a partner with God in the "creating and controlling of worlds" through his creative discerning and application of the Halakhah from which he draws his sense of self and of importance. Though halakhic man is humble before his Creator, he also recognizes his own greatness due to the important role he plays in bringing God's creation to full fruition.

Chapter Fourteen

The Religious Ecstasy of Halakhic Man

Rabbi Soloveitchik addresses the issue of religious passion and the love of God that may at first glance appear to be wanting in the highly analytic and normative perspective halakhic man in comparison to the strong emotional nature of *homo religiosus*.

> Is halakhic man devoid of the splendor of that raging and tempestuous sacred, religious experience that so typifies the ecstatic homo religiosus?...Is it possible for halakhic man to achieve such emotional exaltation that all his thoughts and senses ache and pine for the living God? (HM, p. 83)

The Rav explains that the ecstatic religious experience of halakhic man exceeds the intensity of that of *homo religiosus*. However, where the *homo religiosus's* experience is a direct and intuitive one that is not necessarily based on a prior intellectual experience, halakhic man's passion for God emerges from his prior involvement and mastery with God's revealed law – the Halakhah. The Rav writes:

> Halakhic man is worthy and fit to devote himself to a majestic religiosus experience in all its uniqueness, with all its delicate shades and hues. However, for him such a powerful, exalted experience only follows upon cognition, only occurs after he has acquired knowledge of the a priori, ideal Halakhah and its reflected image in the real world. But since this experience occurs after rigorous criticism and profound penetrating reflection, it is that much more intensive. (Ibid.)

Rabbi Soloveitchik draws a parallel between halakhic man's post-analytic passion for God and that of the physicist who, following his or her mathematical investigation of the cosmos, experiences the wonder and awe of the universe with an quality and intensity not available to one that has not gone through this process of intensive study and mastery of the law.

> To what may the matter be compared? To the physicist who concerns himself with mathematical formulae, the laws of mechanics, the laws of electromagnetic phenomena, optics, etc., etc. He joins together "precept to precept...line to line" (Isa. 28:10, 13), number to number; he engages in complex and difficult calculations, involving the manipulating of ideal, mathematical quantities that, at first glance, are wholly lacking in the music of the living world and the beauty of the resplendent cosmos. (Ibid.)

The Rav is dispelling the general notion that a person who is deeply involved with the analytic process and its atomization of the object of analysis is somehow "shut out" from the ecstatic feeling of awe that one derives from experiencing the whole associated with the generalized intuitive experience. For example, if one deeply analyzes his or her feelings of love towards another, the idea is that this analytic process will somehow diminish the intensity of the emotional experience. This may be the case in certain situations, but with regard to the love of God which is built, to a great degree, on a recognition of the level of complexity and order of this creation, the analysis only intensifies the sense of wonder. This is true for the great scientist and as well for the halakhic man. He writes:

> Did not Newton delight in the beauty of the world when he discovered the law of gravity, or, simultaneously, with Leibnitz, the differential and integral calculus?...From the midst of the order and lawfulness we hear a new song, the

song of the creature of the Creator, the song of the cosmos to its Maker...Not only the qualitative world bursts forth in song, but so does the quantitative world. From the very midst of the laws there arises a cosmos more splendid and beautiful than all the works of Leonardo da Vinci and Michelangelo. Perhaps these experiences of cognitive man are lacking in the emotional dynamic and turbulent passion of aesthetic man; perhaps these experiences are devoid of flashy and externally impressive bursts of ecstasy of stychic enthusiasm. However they are possessed of a profound depth and a clear penetrating vision...So it is also with halakhic man. His religious experience is mature and ripe when he cognizes the world through the prism of the Halakhah...At times we may tend to look askance upon that religiosity which follows cognition, for does it not seem somewhat pallid, overly refined, and indeed fastidious? However these characteristics are in truth a highly auspicious sign. Halakhic man, also, after he has perfected his ideal world with laws, statutes, judgments, decrees, stringencies, legal detail, and particulars, does not remain fastened to the realm of the particulars, does not remain fastened to the realm of the particular but betakes himself to the realm of the universal, to the idea of wholeness. (HM, p. 84-85)

The "Sin" of Overlooking the Particulars

Rabbi Soloveitchik goes further than just defending the validity of the halakhic man's religious passion. He finds the religious experience of those who forgo the analytic, intellectual dimension of the religious experience and choose a "direct approach" through which they attempt to "storm the gates" and seek an intimate merging with God, lacking in depth. He writes regarding the weakness of the pre-analytic religious experience when compared to the one that is preceded by a deep intellectual stage:

> They (the post-analytic experience) do not flourish and then wither away like experiences that are only based upon a vague, obscure moment of psychic upheaval. Such an experience is not some fleeting, unstable phenomenon that ebbs and flows, but is fixed and determined, possessed of a clear and flimsy established countenance of its own. (HM, p. 84)

The "lover of nature" without a scientific understanding of nature cannot, the Rav explains, cannot experience natural beauty with the depth and intensity of one who understands the underlying structure. The inspired religious personality cannot experience or attach to God with the same intensity and depth as one who has devoted one's attention to the study of the law and revealed will of God. For the Rav, analysis and study do not dilute the experience of the whole, but instead deepen and enhance its power.

How Halakhah Deepens the Religious Experience for Halakhic Man

Rabbi Soloveitchik expresses the Halakhah as the "royal road" to drawing close to God. The Halakhah is "imprinted" so to speak, with the a Godly character and, as such, is the lens by which halakhic man perceives, to his highly limited ability, the nature of God, and by which he establishes his living relationship with the Creator. The Rav writes:

> The approach to God is also made possible by the Halakhah. Primarily halakhic man cognizes God via His Torah, via the truth of halakhic cognition. There is truth in the Halakhah, there is a halakhic epistemology, there is a halakhic thinking "the measure thereof is longer than the earth" (Job 11:09). There is a Torah wisdom "that is broader than the sea (ibid).

And all of these are rooted in the will of the Holy One, blessed be He, the revealer of the Law. (HM, p. 85-86)

Halakhic Man – A Man of Few Words

Rabbi Soloveitchik continues his portraying of halakhic man by describing how careful and decidedly minimalistic he is with regard to language and expression. Halakhic man does not seek to create poetic and beautiful verbal presentations of his thoughts and feelings. His focus is more on clarifying and refining his thinking - the creative and analytic process of understanding of the Halakhah. His objective with regard to spoken or written words is to communicate these insights in the most efficient and concise manner, imbuing his few words with layers of meaning and ideas. He has no need or desire to enthrall or inspire with his words. Words are the servants of ideas and communicating these ideas is their sole function. Great exemplars of this approach include Rashi, Maimonides and the Vilna Gaon. The Rav writes:

> Halakhic man is not a man of words…Every jot and tittle of Rashi's commentary on the Talmud and Maimonides Mishneh Torah alludes to heaps and heaps of halakhot…Each and every sentence in the writing of R. Hayyim constitutes a flowing spring of creative insight and cognition. (HM, p. 87)

Rabbi Soloveitchik contrasts this approach to the beautiful poetic expression of the *homo religiosus* and he portrays this as sacrificing precision for expressiveness. He writes:

> When ecstasy seizes hold of homo religiosus, he bursts forth in song and psalm and is very casual with the phrases and linguistic forms he uses. Halakhic man, on the contrary, is very sparing in his recitation of piyyutim, not, heaven forbid, on account of philosophical qualms, but because he serves his

Maker with pure halakhic thought, precise cognition, and clear logic. He does not waste his time reciting songs and hymns. The cognition of the Torah-this is the holiest and most exalted type of service. (HM, p. 87)

Then the Rav relates a personal event in which this idea is expressed quite dramatically:

Once my father (Rav Moshe Soloveitchik-RB) entered the synagogue on Rosh Ha-Shanah, late in the afternoon, after the regular prayers were over, and found me reciting Psalms with the congregation. He took away my Psalm book and handed me a copy of the tractate Rosh Hashanah. "If you wish to serve the Creator at this moment, better study the laws pertaining to the festival." (Ibid)

Halakhic Man's Learning Torah *Lishmah*

One of the highest ideals of Judaism is the concept of learning Torah "for its own sake" (*Torah lishmah*). Rabbi Soloveitchik clarifies the meaning of this term for halakhic man, contrasting it to the perspective that *homo religiosus*. While for *homo religiosus*, *Torah lismah* means the learning of Torah for the sake of cleaving to God, in his continual attempt to draw closer and merge with the Creator, for halakhic man it simply means to learn Torah for the sake of clarification and understanding of the Torah itself. For halakhic man is no higher purpose. The Rav writes:

The whole notion of (Torah) lishmah ('for its own sake' or 'for the sake of the (Divine) Name' primarily to (studying) for the sake of the love of the Torah-i.e., that one should exert oneself to determine the root principle (of the law). But a person may think that *lishmah* means (for the sake of) cleaving (to God), and, therefore, according to this opinion it would be preferable for one to occupy oneself with songs and hymns and in particular with the Psalms of (David,) the sweet singer of Israel, that arouse in one's love for God and a sense of His closeness, and this is sufficient for him and in this manner he will attain a pleasant life. But such is not the case. For the Midrash (on Psalms 1:8) states that King David requested that God should account one who would recite the Psalms as being on the same level as one who studies the laws of leprosy and tents. This clearly implies that the study of these laws is of more value than the recitation of Psalms. And there is no indication (in the Midrash) that God granted him his request. This is so because the primary purpose of study is not to study simply for the sake of cleaving to God, but to comprehend, through the Torah, the commandments and laws, and to know each and every matter clearly, both its general principles and its particulars…Thus one should study these matters-i.e., these laws-for the sake of the matters themselves.

Chapter Fifteen

Halakhic Man – Consistent, Courageous and Just

In the final chapter of Part I of the essay, Rabbi Soloveitchik concludes with the description of a number of traits characteristic of halakhic man. The Rav interestingly begins with a discussion of the intolerance halakhic man has of those religious individuals who do not exert themselves in an effort to master the Jewish law. Religious fervor without knowledge is held in low esteem by halakhic man. Without a clear understanding of the Halakhah, the nature of a religious life is considered hollow by halakhic man and lacking in the essential quality necessary to understand and actualize God's will in the world. He writes:

> Piety that is not based upon knowledge of the Torah is of no consequence in his view. There can be no fear of God without knowledge and no service of God without the cognition of halakhic truth. "A crude man fears not sin, nor is a man ignorant of the Torah pious" (Avot 2:5). The old saying of Socrates, that virtue is knowledge, is strikingly similar to the stance of halakhic man. (HM, p. 89)

Although there are many who would be considered in the category of *homo religiosus* who are masters of the Halakhah as well, there are also those who are seen as religious luminaries based primarily on their fervor or mastery of expression. It is this second group that halakhic man disparages. One can never, from the point of view of halakhic man, vault over this step of mastery of the law and reach heights of religious ecstasy and attachment due to a powerful intuition or religious fervor.

Halakhic Man Places No Objective Above the Halakhah

In the hierarchy of values of the halakhic man, the understanding and actualizing of the Halakhah stands at the pinnacle. The Halakhah will not be compromised or altered in any way for some political, personal or other consideration, regardless of the issue at stake or the well-meaning intentions of the competing value. The Halakhah is the righteousness and mercy of God through which man's life obtains its value. There is nothing for the halakhic man that can compete or compare with it. The Rav writes:

> He (halakhic man-*RB*) will not overlook a single jot or tittle of the Halakhah, even to realize some lofty desire. We have here manifested not the religious zeal of the universal *homo religiosus* but a type of zeal specific to the halakhist-the zeal for the truth, granted him by the Almighty. Thus, halakhic man will not be overly lenient; but, at the same time, he will not be overly strict. The truth will call to account those who dishonor it, be they extreme rigorists or extreme permissivists...Halakhic man implements the Torah without any compromises or concessions, for precisely such implementation, such actualization is his ultimate desire, his fondest dream. When a person actualizes the ideal Halakhah in the very midst of the real world, he approaches the level of that godly man, the prophet-the creator of worlds.

The Profound Courage of Halakhic Man

The unique singularity of purpose of halakhic man makes him immune to the psychological and environment pressures that often cause others to compromise on their ideals. Halakhic man, having no particular need for recognition or wealth, is not influenced by those with power. His holy mission to actualize God's will in the world gives halakhic man a quiet courage that allows him to stand up to intense pressures and not be moved from his purpose of actualizing the justice and mercy which are at the core of the Torah's system of laws. In this regard he is the passionate defender of the poor and the weak, as God has commanded. Rabbi Soloveitchik writes:

> The rich are deemed as naught in his view. He is the father of orphans, the judge of widows. Mr. uncle, R. Meir Berlin (Bar Ilan), told me that once R. Hayyim of Brisk was asked what the function of a rabbi is. R. Hayyim replied: "To redress the grievances of those who are abandoned and alone, to protect the dignity of the poor, and to save the oppressed from the hands of his oppressor." Neither ritual decisions nor political leadership constituted the main task of halakhic man. Far from it. The actualization of the ideals of justice and righteousness is the pillar of fire which halakhic man follows, when he, as a rabbi and teacher in Israel, serves his community. More, through the implementation of the principles of righteousness, man fulfills the task of creation imposed upon him: the perfection of the face of creation. (HM, p. 91).

The Moral Consistency of Halakhic Man

Rabbi Soloveitchik explains that absolute moral consistency is a fundamental characteristic of halakhic man. Many religionists draw a bold line between their religious persona which they present to God in the house of worship and in prayer. Before God they are full of lofty ideals and profess profound humility. But their worldly personae are quite different - often aggressive, appetitive and insensitive, emerging when they conduct business or seek to satisfy a particular materialistic or hedonistic desire. Not so with halakhic man. He has one face and one persona that are consistent in all situations. There is no distinction in his approach to fulfilling the commandments between him and God as opposed to those which govern his behaviors towards his fellow. He does not approach the Halakhah differently whether it is a law of how to conduct the Yom Kippur service or how to conduct a business deal. Both are equally bound by halakhic directives and both are carried out meticulously in adherence to these directives. The Rav writes:

> The universal homo religiosus not infrequently sets up markers and draws sweeping demarcation lines-till here is the divine-heavenly-transcendental realm and from this point on the realm of earthly, bodily life. Homo religiosus, praying is his house of worship, prostrated on the cold stone floor, repeating over and over the old litany, non mea sountas sed tua fiat-not my will be done, only Thine-is not at that moment a this-worldly man, possessor of riches and chattels, estates and factories, who drives his impoverished workers ruthlessly, and whose hands are often stained with the blood of the outcast and the ill-gotten gain wrung from the hands of the unfortunate...Halakhah, however, rejects such a personality split, such a spiritual schizophrenia. It does not differentiate between the man who stands in his house of worship, engaged in ritual activities, and the mortal who must wage the arduous battle of life. The Halakhah declares that man stands before God not only in the synagogue but also in the public domain, in his house, while on a journey, while lying down and rising up...The marketplace, the street, the factory, the house, the meeting place, the banquet hall, all constitute the backdrop for the religious life. The synagogue does not occupy a central place in Judaism. (HM, p. 93-94)

The Rav points out the departure of liberal Judaism from this seamless consistency of halakhic man, when it attempts to restrict religious activity to the house of worship and exile it from the day to day activities of everyday life. He writes:

> When liberal Judaism expelled the *Shekhinah*, the Divine Presence, from the broad arena of Jewish life, it set aside a special place for it in the temple. As a result, according to the liberal Jewish outlook the temple stands at the heart of religion. The Halakhah, the Judaism that is faith to itself, however, which brings the Divine Presence into the midst of empirical reality, does not center about the synagogue or study house. These are minor sanctuaries. The true sanctuary is the sphere of our daily, mundane activities; for it is there that the realization of the Halakhah takes place. (HM, p. 94-95)

Understanding Halakhic Man

Part II

His Creative Capacity

Halakhic Man Part Two-Introduction

Rabbi Soloveitchik divided his essay into two parts. The second section is titled "Halakhic Man-His Creative Capacity" and focuses on the centrality of intellectual creativity in the act of learning and interpreting the Torah. The Torah scholar does not receive the Torah as a finished and perfect product, but one that God has given to man to collaborate upon as a co-creator in his role of delving into its depths and then interpreting and applying its laws and directives to the world. This is a highly creative act and one in which man fulfills God's will that man should "walk in His ways." Just as God creates, man creates. Together they create the Torah. God left the Torah and world, so to speak, "incomplete" so that man could complete the holy task of creation which He began.

The Rav extends the locus of man's creative impulse to man himself. Through the act of reflection and repentance, a human being is charged with the act of creating and recreating him or herself. Here too, God does not create a finished product or one that will grow to completion without any creative input from man. Repentance is the act of self-creation in which the person builds and rebuilds himself to refine and develop his human capacities to become more than he was and to repair that which he has damaged and distorted through sin.

The creative nexus of halakhic man consists of three areas:

1-creativity in the area of Halakhah formulation of the ideal halakhah.

2-creativity in the application of the Halakhah to the world in order to repair it and bring it to fruition as a human civilization operating with justice and mercy.

3-creativity in the act of personal repentance and refinement to complete the process of creating oneself "in the image of God".

In the five chapter of Part Two, the Rav will explore these areas and integrate the role of creativity into the profile he has presented in Part One of the essay. There are some who believe that there can be too much emphasis on the creative aspects of Torah learning. After all, as a servant of God, isn't our core role to obey God without question? Doesn't this role of being an obedient servant minimize the importance of our own creative input regarding the structure of the law?

It is, in part, because of this prominent view of the pious individual, that the Rav goes to such lengths to emphasize the centrality of creativity in the life of the halakhic man. We are the servants of God and the halakhic man is a lover a God whose greatest desire is to do His will. But unlike other masters who create and rule over subjects for the good of the master, God creates and rules over His subjects to bring out the best in them. In being creative in the areas that the Rav describes, halakhic man is carrying out the absolute will of God. This creative life is the life that God "desires" of man and there is no conflict between obedience to the King and maximizing creativity in the learning of Torah and the exploration and refinement of the self. This is creativity in the service of God.

Chapter One

Obedient Creativity

Obedience and creativity are usually viewed as polar opposites. Why? Usually the obedient person has been given a task by the master which needs to be carried out precisely and with minimal variation. Was creativity valued in the Hebrew slaves of Egypt as they labored to build the storage cities of Pharaoh? Creativity is not usually valued in a slave, a servant or a manual worker. Is not the Halakhah a precise set of instructions which the obedient servant of God (*eved Hashem*) needs to faithfully carry out without question, without input? At first glance, it may seem so. But, Rabbi Soloveitchik explains, the study and fulfillment of the Halakhah, although a system of strict obedience to God, is at the same time a gloriously creative activity! How is this so? He writes regarding the creative study of the Torah and the creative implementation of Torah law in the world:

> Halakhic man is a man who longs to create, to bring into being something new, something original. The study of Torah, by definition, means gleaning new, creative insights from the Torah (*hiddushei Torah*)...This notion of *hiddush*, of creative interpretation, is not limited solely to the theoretical domain but extends as well into the practical domain, into the real world. The most fervent desire of halakhic man is to behold the replenishment of the deficiency in creation, when the real world will conform to the ideal world and the most exalted and glorious of creations, the ideal Halakhah, will be actualized in its midst. (HM, p. 99)

The system of Halakhah is God's greatest gift to man's creative impulse. An in-depth study of the law reveals an endless source of insight and wisdom of the Divine Mind which requires the creative input of the human mind to understand and apply its intricacies to theoretical cases and to actualize them in the myriad situations that arise in the world. This is creative obedience. This creative dimension of the halakhic man takes on a special exaltedness as it is a partnership with the Creator in the building and completion of His worlds. Human creativity, especially in the area of halakhah, but also more generally, is a holy act because through it man "walks in the ways of God" as the Torah commands him. This creative involvement in the Halakhah, both in its study and actualization, are at the core of Judaism. The Rav writes:

> The dream of creation is the central idea in the halakhic consciousness-the idea of the importance of man as a partner of the Almighty in the act of creation, man as creator of worlds...And if at times we raise the question of the ultimate aim of Judaism, of the telos of the Halakhah in all its multifold aspects and manifestations, we must not disregard the fact that this wondrous spectacle of the creation of worlds is the Jewish people's eschatological vision, the realization of all its hopes. (HM, p. 99).

The Halakhic Nature of the Entire Torah

Rabbi Soloveitchik explains that the entire corpus of the written and oral Torah is viewed by halakhic man as the source material for formulating the law. His creativity addresses this process. Even those areas of the Torah that seem to be wholly narrative in character or addressing areas of wisdom that appear far from Jewish law are viewed creatively and accurately in a halakhic context. The Rav writes:

> The Halakhah sees the entire Torah as consisting of basic laws and halakhic principles. Even the scripture narratives serve the purpose of determining everlasting law. "The mere conversations of the servants of the fathers are more important than the laws (Torah) of the sons. (Genesis Rabba 60:11)...Our Torah does not contain even one superfluous word or phrase. Each letter alludes to basic principles of Torah law, each word to "well-fastened," authoritative, everlasting halakhot. From beginning to end it is replete with statutes and judgments, commandments and laws. (HM, p. 100)

The Rav dismisses the idea that the Torah is to be compartmentalized into its halakhic, legal content and its other, perhaps for more esoteric and mystical parts. Although I would not say that the Rav rejects these additional dimensions of the Torah, he firmly adheres to the idea that the Torah relates to halakhah and man's obligations to carry out God's will in the world through the study and actualizing of the law. The Rav write regarding the description of the creation of the world in Genesis:

> Therefore, if the Torah spoke at length about the creation of the world and related to us the story of the making of heaven and earth and all their host, it did so not in order to reveal cosmogonic secrets and metaphysical mysteries but rather in order to teach *practical* Halakhah. The Scriptural portions of the creation narrative is a legal portion, in which are to be found basic, everlasting halakhic principles, just like the portion of *Kedoshim* (Lev. 19) or *Mishpatim* (Exod. 21). (HM, p. 100)

In footnote 103, the Rav brings the first Rashi of the book of Genesis as a support for this position. Rashi posits the questions of why the Torah did not begin with Exodus 2:12 where the first clear description of a Jewish law is given, regarding the requirements of viewing month of Nissan as a beginning of the year in regard to certain calculations. In other words, why do we require the narrative of the creation of the world and that of the Avraham, Yitzchak and Yaakov and the brothers, when these do not appear, at first glance, to constitute law? Rashi answers that there is a halakhic matter which required the Torah to begin with the creation of the world:

> What is the reason, then that it begins with (the story of) the beginning? Because (through beginning with the account of creation) 'He hath declared to His people the power of His works (in order) to give them the heritage of the nations' (Ps. 111:6). For if the nations of the world should say to Israel 'You are robbers, for you conquered the lands of the seven nations,' they (Israel) could reply: 'The entire world belongs to the Holy One, blessed be He; He created it and He gave it to them (to the seven nations) and of His own will He took it from them and gave it to us." (HM, footnote 103, p.156)

Rashi, according the Rav, is addressing the question of why, if the Torah is a guide to the norms of halakhah, do we need to include the story of creation? The explanation Rashi provides is that there are normative considerations that are addressed (Israel's legal rights to the conquest of the land that was possessed previously by the Canaanites) by the creation story. Once again, I would caution the reader at jumping to the false conclusion that the Rav dismisses or diminishes the non-halakhic knowledge that the Torah provides. Of course the Torah, as the revelation of God, contains information that is not solely halakhic in character. I believe what the Rav is clarifying is that the essential character of the Torah is halakhic in nature –even for those portions that do not seem to address halakhic issues from a surface reading. Even God's creative act itself, in his bringing the universe into being from nothing, the Rav connects to a halakhic obligation of man. Even the esoteric, non-normative aspects of the Torah have a normative aspect. Man, who is tasked by the law to "walk in ways of God" and to imitate His ways is also obligated to create or perhaps more accurately, co-create a world. The Rav writes:

> If the Torah then chose to relate to man the tale of creation, we may clearly derive one law from this manner of procedure-viz. that man is obliged to engage in creation and the renewal of the cosmos...When God created the world, He provided an opportunity for the work of His hands-man to participate in His creation. The Creator, as it were, impaired reality in order that mortal man could repair its flaws and perfect it. God gave the Book of Creation-that repository of the mysteries of creation-to man, not simply for the sake of theoretical study but in order that man might continue the act of creation. (HM, p. 101).

God's "Creation of Chaos" in the World

Rabbi Soloveitchik now turns to a difficult area-the presence of chaotic, destructive forces in the world which constantly work against and threaten the beauty and holiness of the world. In this portion of the essay the Rav embraces the position of this chaos being an intended creation of God which is continuously challenging those orderly, holy elements. It was from this chaos that God fashioned the world and He allowed a portion of it to remain in existence and empowered, only to be controlled by the holy law. The Rav writes:

> When God engraved and carved out the world, He did not entirely eradicate the chaos and the void, the deep, the darkness, from the domain of His creation. Rather, He

> separated the complete, perfect existence from the forces of negation, confusion and turmoil and set up cosmic boundaries, eternal laws to keep them apart. (HM, p. 102)

Rabbi Soloveitchik cites the Torah's use of the image of the ocean and shore as a potent symbol of this bounded chaos existing in the world. The Halakhah is more than simply a way of life for people to live pleasantly. It is the holy order of the universe which holds back the existential forces of destruction that are part of existence. This dimension adds immeasurably to the esteem which the halakhic man attributes to the Halakhah and his quest to actualize it in the world.

> The sight of a tempestuous sea, of whirling, raging waves that beat upon the shore there to break, symbolizes to the Judaic consciousness the struggle of the chaos and void with creation, the quarrel of the deep with the principles of order and the battle of confusion with the law. (HM, p. 102)

Rabbi Soloveitchik portrays this chaotic element of God's world as a willful one that desires and plots to break through its boundaries and envelop the orderly and beautiful elements of existence, returning them to the void from which they came. It is similar to the physical laws of entropy in which all physical matter tends towards disorder unless energy is exerted to prevent it. In the spiritual realm, the Rav explains, there is a similar situation. A constant battle rages between the forces of chaos and injustice and those of order, holiness and justice. The battle is fought through the Halakhah and the brave, undaunted battle of the halakhic man to impose this holy order onto the world.

> Thus the deep desires to burst out of the enclosures of the law and shatter the reams of orderly creation, the cosmic process, the regular course of the world, and plunge them all back into "nothingness," into desolation and ontic emptiness. However it is held firm in the grip of the mighty law and its principles. (HM, p. 104-105).

One could ask why this "battle against chaos" of the halakhic man is included in Part II of the essay which focuses specifically on the creativity of halakhic man. Although the Rav does not state it explicitly, I would speculate that the Rav is explaining the level of challenge that the halakhic man is facing. Halakhah is not simply a way of life. It is an ongoing war with a powerful and intelligent foe. Chaos manifests itself in the world through those evil individuals and nations who have decided to devote their energies and talents to work against the establishment of justice and mercy. As we have seen in the history of Jewish people and humanity in general, these are formidable foes. Without a powerful, bold creativity in understanding the depths of the law and applying it with precision to the world, the forces of order and justice cannot prevail and chaos will overtake its boundaries and envelope the world. Creativity in the Halakhah is not simply a praiseworthy, laudable quality-it is a necessity in order for halakhic man to maintain the world and triumph over his evil foes.

If I could take a moment to bring a *mushal*, imagine an evil regime such as the Nazis, which threatened to return the world to the chaos of cruelty and injustice. The Allies (U.S, England, France, etc.) were tasked with pushing back against this expanding chaos and returning it to its restricted place in the world. But in order to do this, the Allies had to develop weapons and strategies that would defeat the formidable army of the Third Reich. The American scientists and leaders had to understand the materials and forces of nature, materials and human psychology and apply this knowledge creatively to formulate the weapons and strategies that would defeat their foe. The halakhic man also must delve deeply into the knowledge of the Torah and understand the holy material deeply. He must then creatively apply this knowledge to the "battle at hand" to defeat the ever-present forces of chaos, evil and injustice that are constantly working to expand their empire in the world.

Chapter Two

Creativity, Holiness and the Blessing on the New Moon

In this chapter Rabbi Soloveitchik continues his discussion of the role of creativity in the life of halakhic man, the Jewish people and humanity in general. He describes how the text of the Jewish blessing on the new moon expresses the manner through which God has implanted an essential role for creativity within His creation and how this creativity brings holiness to the world. On the one hand, blessing on the moon bring to man's mind the orderly, lawful nature of the creation and its governance by natural laws. But additionally, the blessing notes the cycle of moon from thin crescent to full moon and back again to crescent as a symbol of defectiveness and renewal, which it relates to the place of the Jewish people in the history of the world and its future redemption. The moon becomes a rich and complex symbol of perfect orderliness of the world and, at the same time, a symbol of its unfulfilled, unfinished nature. The Rav writes:

> The Jewish people see in the orderly and lawful motion of the moon in its orbit a process of defectiveness and renewal, the defectiveness of the creation and its renewal, it replenishment. They, therefore, whisper a strange silent prayer: "May it be Thy will...to replenish the defect of the moon so that there be in it no diminution. And let the light of the moon be like to light of the sun, like the light of creation, like it was before it was diminished. (HM, p. 106)

According to the *midrash*, the sun and moon were originally equal in their luminosity, but the moon was diminished as a punishment for its wanting to be the sole source of light. God "compensated" this loss of the moon and "comforted" it with the new moon blessing. The *midrash* in question appears in *Chulin 60b* and in *Bereishit Rabba*:

> Rabbi Shimon ben Pazi said: Two verses contradict one another: "And God created the two great luminaries" [Gen 1:16], and it is written, "the great light... and the small light" [ibid.]. The moon said before the Holy One blessed be He: Master of the Universe, can two kings wear one crown? He said to her: Go and diminish yourself. She said before Him: Master of the Universe, because I said a proper thing before You, must I diminish myself?! He said to her: Go and rule over the day and the night. She said to Him: Of what benefit is a candle in bright daylight? Of what benefit can I be? He said: Let Israel count days and years by you. She said to Him: the day is also impossible, nor are tekufot counted according to me. As is written: "and they [i.e., both the sun and the moon] shall be for seasons and appointed times, for days and years" [ibid. 1:15]. [He said:] Go and let the righteous be called by your name—Jacob the Small [Amos 7:5], Samuel the Small [1 Sam 2:19], David the Small [1 Sam 16:11, 17:14].

The Midrash and the new moon blessing are not speaking of an astronomical change in which the moon and sun will somehow alter their actual structure and function. Instead, as the premier symbols of God's orderly creation of the world, they are communicating an idea about the development of human history and the eschatological (messianic) perspective of the Torah. Yes, it is true that the physical order has a beauty and perfection in the precision of its laws. But do not think that this physical aspect of creation is its completion, or even it's essence. The creation of God stands in a diminished state. Until it has been fully infused with holiness-until knowledge of God, justice and mercy are the order of human existence; the creation of the world has not come to its fruition. The Rav writes:

Examining matters from this esoteric vantage point, the Jewish people see their own fate as bound up with the fate of existence as a whole, that existence which is impaired and cleft asunder by the forces of negation and "nothingness." Physical reality and spiritual-historical existence –both have suffered greatly on account of the dominion of the abyss, of chaos and the void, and their fates parallel one another. When the historical process of the Jewish people reaches its consummation and attains the heights of perfection, then (in an allegorical sense) the flaws of creation as a whole will also be repaired. "He bade the moon renew itself for those who were burdened from birth, who like her will be renewed and will extol their Creator on account of the name of His glorious kingdom" (from the blessing over the new moon). (HM, p. 107)

How Man "Atones" for God

Rabbi Soloveitchik cites a dramatic example of the Torah's recognition of the chaotic, unfinished aspect of world which God has left for man to complete. In continuing to explore the blessing of the new moon the Rav quotes the Talmud, in which God is spoken of as needing to "atone" for the diminishment of the moon mentioned earlier. What is God, so to speak, "atoning" for? The chaos, the evil he left to remain in His world. Why did He not finish the perfection of His world, when, in His omnipotence He had this option? He desired man to complete the world through his own free will and understanding. The Rav writes:

> Man is obliged to perfect what his Creator "impaired." "Resh Lakish said: Why is the new-moon goat offering different, in that (the phrase) 'a sin offering unto the Lord' (Num. 28:15) is used in connection with it (whereas ordinarily the phrase 'a sin offering' is used without the additional 'unto the Lord'? Because the Holy One, blessed be He, said: "This goat shall be an atonement for My diminishing the moon (i.e., it is as if the sin offering is not 'unto the Lord' but 'on behalf of the Lord'."

(Shavu'ot 9a). The Jewish people bring a sacrifice to atone, as it were, for the Holy One, blessed be He, for not having completed the work of creation. The Creator of the world diminished the image and stature of creation in order to leave something for man, the work of His hands, to do, in order to adorn man with the crown of creator and maker. (HM, p. 107)

Creativity and the Realization of Holiness

Rabbi Soloveitchik returns to the analysis of holiness and its relationship to creativity. As the Rav has written earlier in the essay, halakhic man seeks to bring holiness into the earthly world by the realization of the ideal halakhah within it. Unlike the *homo religiosus* that seeks escape from the physical world to exist with God in a higher, purer realm, halakhic man wishes to live his earthly life in a holy manner by investing it with God's law. The Rav now adds to this idea the central role of halakhic man's creativity in realizing this objective. This actualizing of halakhah in the world is halakhic man's ultimate creative act. It is not simply an application of a fixed law to human affairs that constitutes the effort of overcoming the chaos and evil that exists and the bringing of holiness to the world. It is the creative insight and bold intellectual efforts that man must involve himself in to bring the Halakhah to fruition. Not only God's creation, but also man's creativity is now understood as being essential for holiness to exist in the world. The Rav writes:

> Now, however, in the light of the idea of creation stored up in the treasure-house of Halakhah, this outlook on holiness takes on additional dimensions. The dream of creation finds its resolution in the actualization of the principle of holiness. Creation means the realization of the ideal of holiness. The nothingness and naught, the privation and the void are rooted

in the realm of the profane; the harmonious existence, the perfected being are grounded in the realm of holiness.

Man himself, if he want to be holy to God, must create. It is creativity which brings holiness to the world and to the human personality as well. The Rav continues:

> If man wishes to attain the rank of holiness, he must become a creator of worlds. If a man never creates, never brings into being anything new, anything original, then he cannot be holy unto God. That passive type who is derelict in fulfilling his task of creation cannot become holy. Creation is the lowering of transcendence into the midst of our turbid, coarse, material world; and this lowering can take place only through the implementation of the ideal Halakhah in the core of reality.

Halakhah=Contraction=Holiness=Creation

The Rav caps this analyses with an actual equation: halakhah=contraction=holiness=creation. We can break down and examine each equivalence in the equation:

Halakhah=contraction: The Rav has explained that the Halakhah (the Jewish legal system) is God's method of bringing the infinite creations of wisdom, justice, mercy, and beauty into the finite world we live in. The infinite, so to speak, was contracted and concretized by God in the Halakhah.

Contraction=holiness: It is through this process of contraction, most dramatically illustrated in the act of Moses receiving the Torah (i.e., the Halakhah) from the infinite realm of God and bringing it down into the finite realm of the world that bestowed holiness upon the world.

Holiness enters the world through the actualizing of the ideal Halakhah into the activities of humankind.

Holiness=creation: The Halakhah is not bestowed upon humanity as a gift to be opened and enjoyed as is. Instead the Halakhah is an incomplete system which requires man, through his creative intellectual work and concentrated efforts, to master and apply it to the world. This requires not only logic, memory and accuracy, but also creative intellectual work. The halakhic man must be creative in his approach to studying the law to see its subtle meanings and to discover how to correctly apply the Halakhah to a myriad of complex and varied situation that arise in his world. It is only through this creative intelligent human effort that the holiness of the Halakhah emerges.

Man as the Source of Holiness and Chaos and the Creator of Himself

The Rav concludes this chapter with a discussion of the unique range of man's potential forms. A human being can become a vehicle of holiness in the world, joining with God in the process of completing His creation. On the other hand, man can choose to be a source of evil, using his mind and energies to enhance the destructive elements of the void and bring chaos, falsehood, horror, and injustice to the world. Rabbi Soloveitchik writes:

> Judaism declares that man stands at the crossroads and wonders about the path he shall take. Before him there is an awesome alternative-the image of God or the beast of prey, the crown of creation or the bogey of existence, the noblest of creatures or a degenerative creature, the image of the man of

God or the profile of Nietzsche's "superman"- and it is up to man to decide and choose. (HM, p. 109)

It is creativity that here too is the essential deciding element. Before man can create worlds and bring holiness into the world, he must create himself. Man is the only being that can create himself and this is in many ways his primary creative task. To make of oneself a "masterpiece" of justice, wisdom, kindness, and mercy. Where is the manual that man can use to build himself? The Halakhah. It is the guide to the creation of man-to the creation of oneself. The Rav concludes:

> Herein is embodied the entire task of creation and the obligation to participate in the renewal of the cosmos. The most fundamental principle of all is that man must create himself. It is this idea that Judaism introduced into the world. (HM, p. 109)

Chapter Three

Creativity and Repentance

Rabbi Soloveitchik continues his explanation of self-creation through an analysis of repentance and its halakhic structure and requirements. The act of repentance requires the recognition and discarding of one's previous character and the creation of a new one. He writes:

> Repentance, according to the halakhic view, is an act of creation – self creation. The severing of one's psychic identity with one's previous "I," and the creation of a new "I," possessor of a new consciousness, a new heart and spirit, different desires, longings, goals-this is the meaning of that repentance compounded of regret over the past and resolve for the future. (HM, p. 110)

The Rav continues at this point with an analysis of the repentance as Jewish law. As we read this section of the essay and follow Rabbi Soloveitchik's reasoning we experience first-hand the process of halakhic creativity that the Rav has described. We can follow the steps of the process here as Rabbi Soloveitchik dissects and reassembles the information from the Torah's verses, the Talmud and the writing of Maimonides in his great code of Jewish law, the *Mishnah Torah*. Let's try to follow the Rav's creation of a *hiddush*, a new halakhic insight, as he brings it to light.

First, the Rav brings a quote from the first halakhah of Maimonides' Book of Repentance (Mishneh Torah), which contains a quote from the Torah's book of Leviticus:

> If a person transgressed any of the commandments of the Torah...then when he repents and turns away from his sin, he

is obliged to confess before God, blessed be He...So, too those who have to bring sin offerings or guilt offerings, when they bring their offering for sins committed in error or willfully, do not obtain atonement through those offerings until they have repented and made a verbal confession as it is written: 'He must confess the sin he has committed' (Lev. 5:5). So, too, those who have to bring sin offerings for sins committed in error or willfully, do not obtain atonement through death or lashes until they have repented and confessed. So, too, one who injures his fellow man or damages his property, even though he pays what he owes him, does not obtain atonement until he confesses and turns aside from ever again acting in such a manner. (Mishneh Torah, Laws of Repentance 1:1)

Now the creative analysis begins! First the Rav notes that Maimonides has written here that repentance requires verbal confession (*viddui*). The Rav writes:

> On the one hand, Maimonides is of the opinion that *viddui*, verbal confession, is an indispensable part of the act of repentance. "He does not obtain atonement until he confesses and repents." (HM, p. 110)

But, the Rav explains, there is a *Baraita* (an authoritative part of the Jewish oral law from the mishnaic period that was not incorporated into the Mishnah itself) that seems to not require this verbal confession to be valid. The Rav continues:

> On the other hand, we find the following statement in the *Baraita*: "If a man says to a woman: 'Be thou betrothed unto me on the condition that I am righteous,' even if he is absolutely wicked she is betrothed, for he may have had thoughts of repentance in his heart. (Kiddushin 49b). (HM, p. 110-111)

You might respond to this seeming contradiction by asserting that Maimonides held a different position on the essential nature of confession in the repentance process than that of the Baraita. But this cannot be so since the Rav states:

> Moreover, Maimonides codifies this law (of the validity of the betrothed woman stated above) in Hilkhot Ishut (Laws of Marriage 8:5, Mishneh Torah). We see from here that verbal confession is not an indispensable part of repentance, and that the mere thought of repentance suffices. This contradiction requires analysis. (HM, p. 111)

As is often said to explain leaps of creative intellectual insight: "a miracle happens here". The problem has been posed to the mind. The Rav now, through an act of intellectual creativity takes a step to resolve the seeming contradiction by presenting a deeper, more complete explanation of the meaning of repentance. It is this process of creative insight in discerning the meaning and application of the Halakhah that Rabbi Soloveitchik has been describing as the essential act of the halakhic man and that which brings holiness down into the world. Here is the creative step taken by the Rav, a halakhic man par excellence:

> But in truth the Halakhah has posited two separate laws, two distinct principles, with reference to repentance and its function. (1) Repentance may serve to divest the sinner of his status as a rasha, a wicked man. (2) Repentance may serve as a means of atonement like other means of atonement-sacrifices, the Day of Atonement, afflictions, death and such like. The lack of verbal confession prevents repentance only from serving as a means of atonement, but it does not prevent it from divesting a sinner of his status as a rasha. (ibid)

The Rav takes a creative step in defining repentance to resolve the seeming contradiction between the case cited where verbal confession (*viddui*) is stated as essential and the case cited where verbal confession is not required. Repentance has two separate components: 1) the removal the status of the individual as a *rasha* (an evil individual) 2) the obtaining of atonement (make reparations for the sin- RB). For the purpose of removing the individual's status as a *rasha*, repentance alone will suffice. However, for the person to obtain atonement from God for the sin both repentance and confession are required.

> The lack of verbal confession prevents repentance only from serving as a means of atonement, but it does not prevent it from divesting a sinner of his status as a *rasha*. Thus if one transgresses a negative commandment, from which the penalty is lashes, excision, or the judicial sentence of death, and thereby becomes ineligible as a witness, he need not make a verbal confession in order to regain his status of eligibility, but it suffices if he simply repents inwardly through regretting his past action and resolving never to sin again. (p. 111)

The Rav bring textual supports for this distinguishing of the difference between removing the status of a *rasha* and the achieving of atonement by citing Maimonides "Laws of Evidence" from the *Mishneh Torah* and the fact that the sinner does not require verbal confession to regain his right to be a witness. He cites different types of sinners who are categorized as *rashaim* and not allowed to serve as witnesses and yet are returned to their status as valid witnesses without repentance being achieved.

"Those who are disqualified by reason of extortion or robbery, even if they subsequently make restitution, and not reinstated (as eligible witnesses) until they have repented, and remain ineligible until it is ascertained that they have reformed from their evil ways. When may usurers be considered to have reformed? When they tear up their notes of their own accord...When may the dice players be considered to have reformed? When they tear up their notes of their own accord..." (Maimonides, Laws of Testimony 12:4-10) The sinner's regaining his status of eligibility as a witness is not at all dependent upon verbal confession, for his being divested of his status as a *rasha* has nothing to do with his obtaining atonement, but is dependent only upon the act of repentance itself consisting of regret and resolve. (HM, p. 111-112)

The Creative Gesture of Repentance

Rabbi Soloveitchik now focuses his attention on the creative dimension of repentance. In essence it is an act in which the human will and the intellect operate in tandem to terminate the previous self and to create a new one. This miraculous capacity of man to create something new and discontinuous with what previously existed is portrayed by the Rav as another profoundly creative act that the human being can accomplish. It should be noted that although not all people can become halakhic men and women with regard to the capacity to delve into the abstract system of the Halakhah and emerge with creative insights (*hiddushim*), the ability to repent and remake oneself is an equally exalted creative act and one that is universally available to us all. The Rav writes:

> The desire to be another person, to be different than I am now, is the central motif of repentance. Man cancels the law of identity and continuity which prevails in the "I" awareness

by engaging in the wondrous, creative act of repentance. A person is creative; he was endowed with the power to create at his very inception. When he finds himself in a situation of sin, he takes advantage of his creative capacity, returns to God, and becomes a creator and self-fashioner. Man, through repentance, creates himself, his own "I". (HM, p. 113).

Repentance of Halakhic Man Differs from that of *Homo Religiosus*

The perspective and objective of *homo religiosus*, regarding repentance is far different from that of halakhic man. In the act of repentance the *homo religiosus* is overwhelmed with a sense of regret and melancholy in which his main focus is on the sin he has committed and the unchangeable reality of this evil act. His repentance focuses on atonement in order to rescue himself from punishment. There is no self-creation of a new self here, but more a begging for forgiveness based on recognition by the *homo religiosus* of his lowliness and sinfulness. Atonement is not deserved as all, but a miraculous act of God's grace only. Rabbi Soloveitchik writes:

> (*Homo religiosus*) views repentance only from the perspective of atonement, only as a guard against punishment, as an empty regret which does not create anything, does not bring into being anything new. A deep melancholy afflicts his spirit. He mourns for the yesterdays that are irretrievably past, the times that have long since sunk into the abyss of oblivion, the deeds that have vanished like shadows, facts that he will never be able to change. Therefore, for *homo religiosus*, repentance is a wholly miraculous phenomenon made possible by the endless grace of the Almighty. (HM, p. 113)

In contrast, halakhic man's repentance is portrayed as a constructive, creative process in which the penitent , though certainly regretful, is portrayed as filled with a sense of concerted, positive development in which the will and intelligence are called upon to recreate him in accordance with the will of God. The past sin is not an irreparable mistake, but one that is still "alive" and can be transformed by repentance into something positive and capable of yielding wondrous outcomes.

The Rav writes:

> Halakhic man does not indulge in weeping and despair, does not lacerate his flesh or flail away at himself...Halakhic man is engaged in self-creation, in creating a new "I." He does not regret an irretrievably lost past but a past still in existence, one that stretches into and interpenetrates with the present and the future...Halakhic man is concerned with the image of the past that is alive and active in the center of his present tempestuous and clamorous life and with a pulsating, throbbing future that has already been "created".

Repentance and the Halakhic Man's View of Time

Rabbi Soloveitchik addresses the view of time (past, present and future) that underlies halakhic man's conception of repentance as described in the essay. Classically speaking the past is viewed as an unalterable fact. What occurred, occurred and cannot be changed by what a person does in the present. Causality moves in one time direction. Similarly, the future is viewed as being non-existent, imagined in the mind of the person but has no actual existence. This classic view of time invalidates the idea of repentance. The Rav writes:

> There is a living past and there is a dead past. There is a future which has not as yet been "created," and there is a future already in existence. There is a past and there is a

> future that are connected with one another and with the present only through the law of causality-the cause found at moment *a* links up with the effect taking place at moment *b*, and so on. However, time itself as past appears only as "no more" and as future appears as "not yet." From this perspective repentance is an empty and hollow concept. It is impossible to regret a past that is already dead, lost in the abyss of oblivion. Similarly one cannot make a decision concerning a future that is as yet "unborn".

Repentance, as understood by the halakhic man utilizes a system of time that differs markedly from that of the one way causality described above. The actions of the present can alter the nature of a past that is still "open" to change. The future can exist within the present as something that take on specific characteristics that can be known and impactful on the here and now. It is this unique perspective on time and the relationship between past, present and future that give repentance its power and meaning. Rabbi Soloveitchik states:

> However, there is a past that persists in its existence, that does not vanish and disappear but remains firm in its place. Such a past enters into the domain of the present and links up with the future. Similarly, there is a future that is not hidden behind a thick cloud but reveals itself now in all its beauty and majesty. Such a future, drawing upon its own hidden roots, infuses the past with strength and might, vigor and vitality. Both past and future-are alive; both act and create in the heart of the present and shape the very image of reality. From this perspective we neither perceive the past as "no more" nor the future as "not yet" nor the present as "a fleeting moment". (HM, p. 114)

The penitent's resolve in the present to separate from sin in the future has the ability to transform the quality of the past event, removing it's sinful character. The Rav presents this mechanism as a real event and not merely an allegorical way of reflecting on the repentance process. He writes:

> The Halakhah declares that the person who returns to his Maker creates himself in the context of a living, enduring past while facing a bright and welcoming future...Sin, as a cause and as the beginning of a lengthy causal chain of destructive acts, can be transformed, underneath the guiding hand of the future, into a source of merit and good deeds, into love and fear of God. The cause is located in the past, but the direction of its development is determined by the future. "Great is repentance, for deliberate sins are accounted to him as meritorious deeds" (Yoma 86b). The sin gives birth to mitzvoth, the transgression to good deeds. (HM, p. 115-116)

Creativity and Causality

Rabbi Soloveitchik reflects on the contradiction between causality, free will and creativity. Causality in which the past irrevocably creates the present and the present the future, does not allow for free will or creativity to play a role in the emergence of reality. The Rav explains:

> Therefore, the creative gesture, of which man is capable, cannot be reconciled with the scientific concept of causality, whether it be prospective or retrospective.

The Rav describes a causality that has many potential outcomes determined by the human creative choice. He continues:

> But it can be reconciled with the principle of causality that is rooted in the type of time consciousness we described earlier. When the future participates in the clarification and elucidation of the past-points out the way it is to take, defines its goals, and indicates the direction of its

> development-then man becomes a creator of worlds. Man molds the image of the past by infusing it with the future, by subjecting the "was" to the "will be". To be sure, each cause gives rise to a new causal sequence. But this sequence can oftentimes head in various directions. It stands at the crossroads and ponders: Whither? If man so desires, it will travel in the direction of eternity; the past will heed his word and attach itself to him. The causes will submit to his directives. (HM, p. 116-117)

It is this perspective on the past, as well as the future, being susceptible to the free and creative actions of the human being that is at the source of the optimistic perspective of the halakhic man, even in the process of repenting his past sins. These too can be altered by the power of repentance if they are infused with a creative effort on the part of the penitent to create a new "I" and abandon the previous one. With a new future now, the past of the penitent also is changed and his sins become transformed into a path to God.

Chapter Four

Rabbi Soloveitchik now describes in some detail halakhic man's perspective on time, expanding on the concepts described in the previous chapter on repentance. The Rav explains that the scope of time in which the halakhic man lives is much wider than that of his own past and future individual life. He lives within the boundless time spectrum of Torah which begins at the first moment of creation and continues through the future redemption when God's world will be brought to full fruition. He writes:

> His time is measured by the standard of our Torah, which begins with the creation of heaven and earth. Similarly, halakhic man's future does not terminate with the end of his own individual future at the moment of death but extends into the future of the people as a whole, the people who yearn for the coming of the Messiah and the kingdom of God. (HM, p. 117-118)

Through the study of the Torah and the fulfillment of its commandments, halakhic man develops his expanded time consciousness. He does not remember the past events or simply believe in the coming of future ones, but instead seeks to experience them and have them leave their impression on his sense of time and of self.

> The whole thrust of the various commandments of remembrance set forth in the Torah-for example, the remembrance of the Exodus, the remembrance (according to Nachmanides) of the revelation at Mount Sinai...the remembrance of the Sabbath day (through the recitation of the *kiddush*), the remembrance of Amalek-is directed toward the integration of these ancient events into man's time consciousness. The Exodus from Egypt, the divine revelation on Mount Sinai, the creation of the world, all are transformed

into an integral part of the content of man's present consciousness, into a powerful direct experience. (HM, p. 118)

The remembrance and experience of the past in the present is an actual halakhic obligation carried out at the annual seder when one recounts and relives the experience of being redeemed from Egyptian bondage. The Rav clarifies:

> The commandment to relate the story of the Exodus carries with it a unique halakhah: "In every generation a man must regard himself as if he came forth out of Egypt" (Pesahim 10:5; cf. Maimonides, Laws of Hametz and Matzah 7:6). But how can a person regard himself as one of those who left Egypt, as a companion of Moses and Aaron in the remote dawn of our history, if not by including himself in this ancient past and in the process of redemption that occurred then? (Ibid)

But all experiences of the past and present by halakhic man are connected to a promised future. The entire process of creation and history which he experiences are tinged with the final redemption in which all events will have their triumphant culmination and the world, history, man, and the Jewish people will achieve fruition. This sense of the future redemption in deeply embedded, as well, in the time consciousness of the halakhic man.

> Not only the infinite past but also the infinite future, that future in which there gleams the reflection of the image of eternity, also the splendor of the eschatological vision, arise out of the present moment, fleeting as a dream. Temporal life is adorned with the crown of everlasting life. (Ibid).

Time and the Experiencing of the *Masorah*

Judaism exists by virtue of the *Masorah*-the Jewish tradition which includes the Jewish law as it has been studied, understood and passed down through the generations, as well as the collected wisdom, tradition and history of the Jewish people. The halakhic man's present is infused with this living tradition of *Masorah*. The Rav often refers to those great scholars of the past with whom he studies and communicates as in his study of Torah. Halakhic man's companions include both those living and dead who participate in the great act of discerning and actualizing God's will in the world.

> The consciousness of halakhic man, that master of the received tradition, embraces the entire company of the sages of the *masorah*. He lives in their midst, discusses and argues questions of Halakhah with them, delves into and analyzes fundamental halakhic principles in their company. All of them merge into one time experience. He walks alongside Maimonides, listens to R. Akiva, senses the presence of Abaye and Raba. He rejoices with them and shares their sorrow...There can be no death and expiration among the company of the sages of the tradition. Eternity and immortality reign here in unbounded fashion. Both past and future become, in such circumstances, ever-present realities. (HM, p. 120)

Fleeting Time vs. Eternal Time

Rabbi Soloveitchik connects a person's perception of time to his sense of life's meaning and value. If a person views the past as dead and gone, the present as fleeting and causally fixed by the past, and the future as a dark unknown, life is experienced as being out of control and possessing a terrifying and meaningless nature.

> Yesterday has already passed, tomorrow is yet to come, and today rapidly descends into the abyss of oblivion. Such a man is subject to the general scientific law of causality-the caused rooted in the past determines the image of the future. His existence does not enjoy the blessing of liberty and free will. The yesterday creates both the now and the tomorrow, and all three deride and mock him. Actions long since gone precipitate deeds yet to come. Life is out of his control. He can create neither himself nor his future. (HM, p. 122)

The Rav contrasts this terrifying profile with the joyous and meaningful one experienced by the halakhic man, due to his experiencing of time in a broader fashion. He lives in the past, present and future and has a sense of his own ability to shape the nature of the present and future through his creative efforts and even to remake his past through the power of repentance.

> He looks behind him and sees a hylic matter that awaits the reception of its form from the creative future. He look ahead of him and confronts a creative, shaping force that can delineate the content of the past and mold the image of the "before". He participates in the unfolding of the causal sequence and the ongoing act of creation. His consciousness embraces the entire historical existence of the Jewish people. Such a time consciousness, whose beginning and end is everlasting life, is the aim of Halakhah and is termed creation-the realization of the eternal Halakhah in the very midst of the temporal, fleeting world, the "contraction" of the glory of the infinite God in the very core of reality, the descent of the everlasting existence into reality circumscribed by the moment.

Halakhic man experiences eternity with the finite moments of living. He "lives" the past, the present and the eternal life of the future within each present moment and, in a sense conquers time and death. Just as the infinite grandeur of God was "contracted" in some mysterious way to be contained with the finite dimensions of the world, infinite time is contracted in the life of the halakhic man and experienced within the finite moments of his days on earth. The Rav concludes this chapter:

> In the midst of the finitude there appear traces or infinity; in the midst of the fleeting moment an ever-enduring eternity. The symbol of this outlook is the idea of repentance, which is identical with true creation. (HM, p. 123)

Creativity is at the source of this time consciousness. It is only through the human creative act that time can be imbued with the eternal dimension described here. Unlike scientific-mathematical time whose impact and effect requires nothing creative from man, the time consciousness of halakhic man requires his creative participation. Without his reflection and repentance the past will remain a dead, unchangeable one. Without his vision, the future will remain a dark, foreboding, oblivion.

Chapter Five

Rabbi Soloveitchik now provides a depiction of halakhic man's view of the individual and his relationship to divine providence and the immortality of the soul. The chapter opens with a discussion of how Maimonides resolves two seemingly contradictory positions. On the one hand, Maimonides clearly holds that what is eternal about man's soul is its connection to universal ideas and concepts. It is through these universals that man cleaves to God and becomes capable of eternal life. The personal and the individualistic aspects of the individual's personality do not seem to have any relevance to eternal life. Aristotle and Plato famously adhered to this position. But yet, our tradition which Maimonides makes clear he is in full agreement with, absolutely maintains that God does provide for individual immortality. But what is it that is *individual* about the immortal aspect of the soul if this immortality is limited to the degree to which it partakes of universal ideas through understanding and merging with them? The Rav states:

> On the one hand, Maimonides subscribed to the view of Aristotle (and Plato) that true, authentic existence is to be found only in the realm of the forms-the universal ideas-while the realm of particularity, rooted in matter (as an individuating principle) does not attain the level of complete being but exists only as an image of the universal. On the other hand, the Halakhah has always insisted upon the principle of individual immortality. How can these two apparently contradictory positions be maintained? (HM, p. 123)

With regard to providence as well, there is a question of whether God's intervention relates to the individual or to the universal of humanity (i.e., humanity considered as a single entity). If God, according to Maimonides, providentially relates only to the universal elements of the man, why would His providence relate to a particular individual and the elements of his personal life? Both the question of the immortality of the soul and the structure of God's providence both turn on a similar question: Is there anything universal in the human being that is also individual and unique to a particular person? The Rav quotes Maimonides' statement from the "Guide for the Perplexed" where he states regarding God's providence:

> For I believe in the lowly world-I mean that which is below the sphere of the moon-divine providence watches only over individuals belonging to the human species and that in this species all the circumstances of the individuals and the good and evil that befall them are consequent upon their deserts, just as it says: 'For all His ways are justice' (Deut. 3:4). But regarding all the other animals, and all the more, the plants and other things, my opinion is that of Aristotle...for all these texts (asserting that there is providence over animals) refer to providence watching over the species and not to individual providence. (HM, p. 124)

The Rav quotes Maimonides' "Mishneh Torah" in a footnote which limits eternal life to righteous individuals, while the wicked (*rasha*) will be "cut off and die". Maimonides writes:

> The good stored up for the righteous is in the world to come, and it is the life unaccompanied by death and the good unaccompanied by evil. The reward of the righteous is that they will attain this bliss and abide in this state of good: the punishment of the wicked is that they will not attain this life but will be cut off and die. He who does not attain this life is the one who is dead, who will never live but in cut off in his

wickedness and has perished like the beasts. (Mishneh Torah, Laws of Repentance, 8:1)

Rabbi Soloveitchik addresses the issue of what is the essential difference between the human being who is under individual providence and who is rewarded with eternal life, as opposed to the one that will be cut off from this bounty and remain undistinguished from the beast. Instead of focusing on the righteous person being observant of the commandments and the wicked one being a person who violates these commandments, the Rav instead distinguishes these two groups by their involvement in the creative gesture. The Rav equates a human being who does not work to create himself in the image of God and to create a world that reflects God's will as a person who fails to establish that human individuality and perhaps remains unredeemed. The Rav states:

> Man, in one respect, is a mere random example of a biological species-species man-an image of the universal, a shadow of true existence. The difference between a man who is a mere random example of the biological species and a man of God is that the former is characterized by passivity, the latter by activity and creation...The man who has a particular existence and not merely a passive, receptive creature but acts and creates. (HM, p. 125)

The human being has the ability to choose to become an individual. This choice to create oneself and ones work is what makes the difference between man as a member of his species versus man as a true individual.

> ...this ontological privilege, which is the particular possession of the man who has a particular existence of his own, a privilege that distinguishes him from all other creatures and endows him with individual immortality, is

dependent upon man himself. He may, like the individual of all other species, exist in the realms of the images and shadows, or he may exist as an individual who is not a part of the universal and who proves worthy of a fixed, established existence in the world of the "forms" and "intellects separate from matter" (Maimonides, Laws of the Foundations of the Torah, 4:9) Species man or man of God, this is the alternative which the Almighty placed before God. (HM, p. 125)

The Rav follows with a lengthy quote from the Maimonides "Guide for the Perplexed in which the point is made that there are many gradations of providence (described as "divine overflow") towards an individual depending on the degree to which a person develops himself and his intellect and transforms himself into a righteous individual.

Accordingly, divine providence does not watch in an equal manner over all the individuals of the human species, but providence is graded as their human perfection is graded...As for the ignorant and disobedient, their state is despicable proportionately according to their lack of this overflow, and they have been relegated to the ranks of the individuals of all the other species of animals: 'He is like the beasts that speak not' (Ps. 49:13,21) (Guide III, 17, 18) (HM, p. 126)

Rabbi Soloveitchik quotes Maimonides extensively here and focuses on his statements describing man's intellectual development as being the primary factor identified regarding whether a person is under God's individual providence and worthy of eternal life. The Rav seemingly adopts this approach, as this section of the text from the "Guide for the Perplexed" and the "Mishneh Torah" constitutes a large portion of this chapter. However, instead of focusing on man's intellect per se as being the deciding factor for providential intervention and everlasting life, the Rav shifts the distinction to one of activity versus passivity, of spontaneity versus receptivity, creativity versus mediocrity. He writes:

> Man at times, exists solely by virtue of the species, by virtue of the fact that he was born a member of that species, and its general form is engraved upon him. He exists solely on account of his participation in the idea of the universal. He himself, however, has never done anything that could serve to legitimate his existence as an individual...He has never created anything, never brought anything into being anything new, never accomplished anything. Never has he sought to render an accounting, either of himself or of the world. Never has he examined himself, his relationship to himself or his fellow man...This is the man as a random example of the biological species. (HM, p. 126-127)

This man who is described as being undistinguished individually from his species is compared to the halakhic man and all those who partake of his nature. The Rav continues:

> But there is another man, one who does not require the assistance of others, who does not need the support of the species to legitimate his existence... His life is replete with creation and renewal, cognition and profound understanding...He recognizes the destiny that is his, his obligation and task in life. He knows that there are two paths before him and that whichever he shall choose there he must go. He is not passive but active. He does not simply abandon himself to the rules of the species but blazes his own individual trail. He is dynamic, not static, does not remain at rest but moves forward in an ever-ascending climb. For indeed, it is the living God for whom he pines and longs. This is the man of God. (HM, p. 127-128)

The Obligation to be Under God's Providence

Rabbi Soloveitchik closes this chapter of the essay by stating the *obligation* of man to become an individual who is under God's providence. The human being, according to the Rav is commanded to become an individual. The existence of God's providence implies for the Rav that a person must strive to avail himself of this wondrous opportunity and become the type of human being who is worthy of having a providential relationship with God. The Rav concludes the chapter:

> The fundamental of providence is here transformed into a concrete commandment, an obligation incumbent upon man. Man is obliged to broaden the scope and strengthen the intensity of the individual providence that watches over him. Everything is dependent on him; it is all in his hands. When a person creates himself, ceases to be a mere species man, and becomes a man of God, then he has fulfilled that commandment which is implicit in the principle of providence. (HM, p. 128)

Chapter Six

The final chapter of Part II and of the essay describes the unique personality of the prophet as the highest level of the individual. Rabbi Soloveitchik follows Maimonides' view in this regard, who held that the prophet represented the pinnacle of human development. The Rav relates this exalted status to the process by which the prophet has participated in his own creation by bringing to full fruition the potential that God gives him. This prophet, the Rav explains should be viewed as a model for our own development. This also echoes the position of Maimonides who has written that each man's goal should be to achieve prophecy by which "the potentiality of the species (man) passes into actuality..." (Guide for the Perplexed, II, 32)

> The most exalted creation of all is the personality of the prophet. Each man is obligated to give new life to his own being by modeling his personality upon the image of the prophet; he must carry through his own self-creation until he actualizes the idea of prophecy-until he is worthy and fit to receive the divine overflow. (HM, p. 128)

In Maimonides' description of the prophet he makes clear that prophecy is the culmination of an intense process of self-development. This act of self-creation is followed naturally by the prophetic vision. The Rav quotes Maimonides' careful description of this process from the "Mishneh Torah":

> It is one of the foundations of religion to know that God causes men to prophesy. Prophecy rests only on an exceedingly wise man, who is strong with respect to his moral habits so that his inclination (*yetzer*) does not overcome him

in anything whatsoever but he, through the use of his mind, always overcomes his inclination, and who also possesses an exceedingly broad and ready mind…he sanctifies himself and withdraws from the path of the generality of the people who walk in the darkness of the times, for he prods himself and teaches his soul not to take any thought at all of any empty matters nor vanities of the age and its contrivances, his mind always facing upward, bound beneath the (celestial) throne, to understand the holy, pure forms, and to behold the wisdom of the Holy One, blessed be He, in its entirety, from the first form until the center of earth, and to know from them His greatness-at once, the Holy Spirit rests upon him. (Mishneh Torah: Laws of the Foundation of the Torah 7:1). (HM, p.129)

The prophecy of God is described as a culmination of general process of human self-development and self-creation. To prepare oneself for prophecy is the most advanced form of this creative process which is on the same spectrum as the self-creative acts of repentance and the achieving of an individual status that bring a person to the level of being worthy of divine providential consideration. The Rav explains this connection:

> In sum, the task of creation with which man is charged is, according to the Halakhah, a triple performance; it finds its expression in the capacity to perform *teshuvah*, to repent, continues to unfold in *hashgahah*, the unique providence which is bestowed upon the unique individual, and achieves its final and ultimate realization in the reality of prophecy and the personality of the prophet. Man starts with repentance, with a fleeting awareness of sin, with the feeling of regret for the past and determination for the future; he continues to exercise his creative powers by searching for individual providence to single him out as an independent personality; and he finally closes and consummates the cycle of creation with attaining the level of prophecy. This is the

path that the Halakhah has charted for man to travel. (HM, p. 130)

Rabbi Soloveitchik fully adheres in this essay, it appears to me, to Maimonides' view of the human being's quest for self-fulfillment having its full culmination in prophecy. The fact that prophecy had not taken place in the past 2500 years, since the last prophet Malachi, does not invalidate or make obsolete this development process or the spectrum of development described. The Jewish tradition makes clear that prophecy will return in the time of the Messiah and, as the Rav has stated in this essay, halakhic man lives with the reality of the past, present and future merging and nurturing one another as a living, vital experience. So for the halakhic man prophecy exists in the present, since his present state of mind and emotions include the realities of the past as well as of the future.

Maimonides' Depiction of Man's Creativity as a Departure from Aristotle

Rabbi Soloveitchik utilizes the conclusion of the essay Halakhic Man to defend Maimonides and to clarify the great philosophical difference that existed between him and Aristotle. The Rav explains that although Maimonides adopted much of Aristotle's positions and terminology they differed in the area of man's creativity, which reflected fundamental distinctions in their respective ontologies (theories of existence). Aristotle held the universe was eternal and that God was not a creator. This perspective removed the role of creativity in Aristotle's view of human development.

> However, a vast abyss separates the view of Aristotle from the ontological outlook of Maimonides, the master halakhist, this despite the fact that the latter uses the terms of the former with respect to this question. First, the whole concept of creation never really took hold in Greek philosophy. As a result of this, Greek philosophy had no room for the true creative act...The pure, first form (*RB*-the Aristotelian view of God) does not create; therefore, man is not obliged to create. (HM, p. 133)

The value of the individual is also foreign to the Aristotelian perspective. Instead, there is a longing for the elimination of the individual aspects of self with an objective of wholly merging with the universal. This too is completely at odds with Judaism's view of individual providence and immortality, as described earlier. The Rav writes:

> The longing for the theoretical life does not consist so much in the realization within the realm of one's own individuality of the potentiality that is latent in matter, as in the abstracting of form from matter. The desire of the theoretical type, according to the view of Plato, Aristotle, and the Stoics, is directed towards complete abstraction and absolute union with the perfect, ultimate realm of universality. The dream of the Attic sage is the obliteration of that particularity which is rooted in matter. Individuality simply cannot exist in the world of a Greek philosopher from any of these schools. (HM, p. 133-134)

The Halakhah's Valuing and Validation of the Individual

Rabbi Soloveitchik now takes a definitive step in his presentation by showing how Judaism is focused on the Halakhah, as opposed to a purely philosophical approach to understanding the world. It is the Halakhah that redeems, elevates and sanctifies the individual. It is the Halakhah which provides the individual with the opportunity of self-creation which effectuates this elevation. The Rav writes:

> Judaism seeks to fortify, strengthen, and ground the reality of the individual, to elevate him to exalted ontological heights. The individual is redeemed by the Halakhah precisely because it leaves the philosophical realm far behind and is thereby able to shape man's personality by means of the new idea of creation which it has introduced to the world. The realm of the universal exists from the very beginnings of creation; the realm of the particular is created by man himself. (HM, p. 134)

Maimonides, the Rav explains, concentrates much of his philosophical focus in the "Guide for the Perplexed" on prophecy as this the ultimate expression of human self-creation and one that is sanctioned and deeply embedded into the Halakhah. The Rav continues:

> Maimonides, in the Mishneh Torah, used the Aristotelian notions of active and passive intellect very sparingly but instead took up at great length the new principle which Judaism brought to light-namely, prophecy and a binding ethical ideal, prophecy as an act of self-creation and self-renewal. (HM, p. 134)

Self-Creation & Liberation from the Universal

It is only when man attains the level of becoming his own unique creation that he is freed from God's universal, species determined structure of lawfulness and enters the domain of providence as an individual. The Rav states:

> Therefore, as long as man has not ascended to the rank of existence where he leaves behind him the domain of the universal and enters into his own personal domain-no longer dependent upon the principles operative in the realm of the universal-he is still subject to the rule of the species and the universal form. However, as soon as he liberates himself from the burden of the species, he becomes a free man. Complete freedom belongs only to the prophet, the man of God. The man who is a mere random example of the species, on the other hand, is wholly under the rule of the scientific lawfulness of existence. Between this species man and the man of God, between necessity and freedom is the middle range in which most people find themselves. Some ascend in the direction of complete freedom; others descend in the direction of complete servitude. (HM, p. 135)

If the individual is successful in fully actualizing his God-given potential and creating himself as a vital, creative individual (the most exalted example of this success being the prophet) he becomes his own unique being, his own species of which there is only one member. It is this new individual that has its own providential relationship with God, just as any species of being would. He is no longer species-man, he is now species-Abraham or species-David or species- (add your own name). The Rav continues:

> Man, initially, must cause all of the potentialities of the species implanted in him to pass into actuality; he must completely realize the form of the species "man." However, once he has actualized this universal form, then, instead of having his own specific image obliterated, he acquires a particular form, an individual mode of existence, a unique personality and an active, creative spirit he leaves behind the domain of the species and enters his own personal domain.

> The realization of the universal in man's being negates any claim that the species has on him. (Ibid).

According to the Rav, Maimonides has combined the Greek process of seeking to refine those aspects of the mind that are connected to universal truths. But unlike the Greeks, this does not extinguish the personal sense of self as the person "merges" with the Universal Mind. Instead, Maimonides augments this process of development with an additional stage: the creation of a new, redeemed individual who defines his own species, is worthy of his own providential oversight and, if he reaches the highest level of development, emerges as a prophet. The Rav writes:

> This outlook is truly striking in its paradoxical nature. It is a hybrid of two views: the view of Aristotle, with its emphasis on the universal, and the view of the Halakhah, with its emphasis on the individual. The method is Greek, the purpose halakhic. The goal of self-creation is individuality, autonomy, uniqueness, and freedom. (Ibid)

Free Will, Halakhah and the Creative Process

Man imitates God as a creator. Just as the universe is an expression of the will, the choice of the Almighty to do so, man creates himself via the process of free will. He chooses (or chooses not) to do so. Although the commandments are structured as a required fulfillment, for the true man of God who has reached the level of individuality, they are not experienced as such. He chooses to obey them as his own personal laws by which he ascends and achieves greater and greater creativity and individuality, as is the will of God. The Rav explains:

> ...the complete freedom of the man of God is embodied in his perception of the norm (i.e., Jewish law-*RB*) as an existential law of his own individual and spiritual independent being; he discovers his freedom in the halakhic principle, which is deeply rooted in his pure soul. For this norm, this principle is unaccompanied by any sense of compulsion, and a person does not feel "as though he were compelled by some mysterious, hidden power." Rather he rejoices in its fulfillment and realization. (HM, p. 135-136)

The human being is provided with free will by God and this is the vehicle by which he completes the creation of himself by actualizing his potential and by which he impacts the world to help bring it to fruition. The will, that ultimately mysterious and impenetrable phenomenon in which man is the primary cause of his own decisions and actions, must be utilized for the species man to become the individual man.

> God created the world for the sake of His will. Therefore, when God apportioned some of His glory to mortal man and bestowed upon him the power of creation, He grounded this creative power in man's will. The will outwits the structured lawfulness of the species; it creates a new, free mode of being in man, one which is not enslaved by the rule of the structured lawfulness of the universal but which it ascends to the very heavens and cleaves to the divine overflow. (HM, p. 137)

The Rav concludes the chapter and the essay with a summation of the nature of halakhic man:

> And halakhic man, whose voluntaristic nature we have established earlier, is, indeed, a free man. He creates an ideal world, renews his own being and transforms himself into a man of God, dreams about the complete realization of the Halakhah in the very core of the world, and looks

forward to the kingdom of God "contracting" itself and appearing in the midst of concrete and empirical reality. (HM, p. 137)

About the Author

Rabbi Richard Borah is a grant writer and non-profit consultant who received smicha in 1991 from Rabbi Yisrael Chait, Rosh Yeshiva of Yeshiva Bnei Torah, in Far Rockaway, New York. Rabbi Borah was the principal of the Torah Academy of Suffolk County in Commack, Long Island and has taught Torah subjects at various education institutions in the New York area. He is the founder of the Observant Artist Community Circle, a non-profit organization focused on developing the nexus between Jewish artists and Jewish scholars. This is Rabbi Borah's 6th book. Previous publications include:

1- Yad on the Yad:14 Essays on Maimonides' Laws of Repentance (2013)
2- Understanding the Lonely Man of Faith: A Guide to Rabbi Joseph B. Soloveitchik's Essay
   (2014)
3- The Rambam and the Rav on the 54 Portions of the Torah
   (2015)
4- Creativity and the Jewish Soul - An Analysis of the 12 Torah Portions of Genesis
   (2016)
5- Creativity and the Jewish Soul- An Analysis of the 11 Torah Portions of Exodus
   (2017)

All of these texts are available at amazon.com.

www.ingramcontent.com/pod-product-compliance
Lightning Source LLC
Chambersburg PA
CBHW061648040426
42446CB00010B/1638